FRANCE

ilbao
UE
ICES   NAVARRE
         Pamplona

Saragossa

ARAGON

CATALONIA

Barcelona

Teruel

Cuenca

VALENCIA

Valencia

BALEARIC ISLANDS

Majorca

ANCHA

MURCIA

Alicante

Murcia

Lorca

Cartagena

RRANEAN SEA

SPAIN

MILES

0   50   100   150

Old Divisions: ············

THE SPANIARD
and the SEVEN DEADLY SINS

Books by Fernando Diaz-Plaja

LITERATURE

ANTHOLOGIES

El amor en las letras españolas
Verso y prosa de la historia de España
Antología del romanticismo español
Teatro español de hoy
Le muerte en la poesía española
La historia en la poesía española

PLAYS

Napoles millonaria, De Filippo (Translated from the Italian)
Macbeth, Shakespeare (Translated from the English)
La visita de la vieja dama, Dürrenmatt (Translated from the German)
Ondina and *No habrá guerra de Troya,* Giraudoux
(Translated from the French)
La reina muerta, Montherlant (Translated from the French)

HISTORY

TEXTS

La historia de España en sus documentos (seven volumes)

BIOGRAPHIES

Guzmán el Malo
Cuando los grandes hombres eran niños . . .
Teresa Cabarrús

GENERAL

La vida española en el siglo XIX.
La vida española en el siglo XVIII.
La Sociedad española (desde 1500).
Griegos y Romanos en la Revolución Francesa.
La vida norteamericana

The SPANIARD
and the
SEVEN DEADLY SINS

by FERNANDO DIAZ-PLAJA

Translated from the Spanish by
JOHN INDERWICK PALMER

CHARLES SCRIBNER'S SONS ▪ New York

Printed in the United States of America
Library of Congress Catalog Card Number 67-21337

End paper map by Ken Fitzgerald

⚈⚈⚈ *CONTENTS* ⚈⚈⚈

Preface   7

PRIDE   *11*

AVARICE   *89*

LUST   *95*

ANGER   *127*

GLUTTONY   *153*

ENVY   *165*

SLOTH   *189*

Epilogue   *213*

Bibliography   *217*

⚞ *Preface* ⚞

THE metaphor is none the less true for being so often repeated. We can't see the forest for the trees. We lose perspective when overwhelmed by detail. To ascertain the shape and extent of the whole we have to go outside it and view it in its entirety, preferably from a hill.

I have tried to find out what this difficult, astonishing, incomparable Spanish forest really is. Going in and out of it, seeing other trees outside which made comparison possible; or, in Spain itself, explaining to foreigners what amazed them, and shocked me as well *after* I had tried to explain it. It is curious how little logic one finds in familiar things and customs when one tries to find reasons for them.

For this book to be born, then, distance was necessary—but physical, not moral distance. The description of Spanish defects does not free me, a Spaniard, from them. To parody the classical phrase, "Nothing that is Spanish is alien to me," and if one of the ways of finding the examples in this book was to strip myself outward, another, equally effective, was to delve into my own inner man. The writer, then, is not a judge; he is rather a witness, and sometimes an accomplice.

Some of the characteristics described in the following pages are common to all peoples called Latin, others to all Europeans; some are simply human. I have not tried to disassociate at every moment those qualities which belong to us by inheritance or those which have reached us by imitation; I attempt to analyze not the historical process but the result.

There is no doubt that the result is unique. The impressive Spanish personality—some aspects of which are hardly mentioned here—astonishes visitors and the few Spaniards who have reflected upon it. It makes an impact on everyone. During my

7

travels I have heard many judgments on our country and have justified, within myself, both the critical and the enthusiastic. What I could not accept was the indifferent comment. "I hate Spaniards" and "I adore Spaniards" are contradictory phrases, but they both have a raison d'être; to hear "Spain isn't bad" disconcerts me, because Spain is strong liquor that may delight or disgust but can never be drunk with the indifference with which we down a glass of water.

Many years ago, in 1951 to be exact, I was passing through London and had a chat with an old friend, Francisco Mayans, who was then in charge of the Spanish Touring Delegation in England. "Why don't you present a trip to Spain as something unique?" I asked. "Why, among the posters urging people to go to France the Beautiful and Italy the Cultured, don't you put up posters saying Yes, but Spain is different?"

Years afterward I was delighted to see the slogan, in fewer words but with the same meaning, everywhere. It is still true. The progressive shrinking of the world, standardizing everything from food to entertainment, from clothes to morals, has not been able to destroy the bulwark of a different Spain.

But be careful with the adjective: being different does not mean—as it is sometimes interpreted—being better. For many years we Spaniards have done nothing but praise ourselves in books, in newspapers, in the cinema, on television, in the theater. Maybe it's as well, after so much flouting of our virtues, for us to meditate a little on our sins.

Especially on the deadly ones.

The Seven Deadly Sins are the most serious that a Catholic can commit. It has seemed to me that, given the extreme importance which Roman Catholicism has had and still has in Spain, it might be interesting to use these sins as a touchstone, to study the special reactions of my compatriots in each case. Because while it is true that "catholic" means "universal," it would be a mistake to believe that the Catholic of Burgos or Valencia reacts the same way to prohibitions or injunctions as the one from Boston or Holland.

For example, most Spaniards are very surprised when someone talks to them of the *Seven* Deadly Sins. The sense of sin exists, even in more dramatic forms than in other countries of the same confession, and the Spaniard is aware of sin even to the point of defying it. But he confines himself to thinking about one sin, that of Lust. His temperament has provoked a greater vigilance on the part of the Church with regard to lust and this, in turn, has made many people think that lust is the only really important sin. Few fail to confess it, but many, on the other hand, forget to tell the priest that they have eaten too much (Gluttony), or have stayed in bed a good while after having slept longer than was necessary (Sloth). (The author does not distinguish a hierarchy among the Deadly Sins; if he grants them unequal space, it is because Spaniards do so.)

These pages follow the courses of the sins but very broadly, dealing more with daily custom than moral theology. In addition to the great Deadly Sins, we study what might be called sub-sins. For example, with Pride we consider vanity, presumption, individualism; with Anger, cruelty and the harshness of customs; with Envy, bitterness and artistic jealousy.

The reader will find a number of Spanish proverbs scattered about the text. A people's proverbs are certainly not, as has been said, samples of its wisdom; they are rather proof of its instincts, which are often pretty low. There are some which are contradictory, others which clinch an idea that has been said before. They are important in every way for understanding a people. A proverb as such is the result of repetition; only when many agree with an expression does it become a proverb, and even when there is another proverb which says the opposite, the first remains as an example of a feeling and as such must be taken into account—even if it is an immoral feeling.

PRIDE

"Pride, as the first in all evil, took the lead. . . . It ran into Spain, the first province in Europe. Spain suited its taste so well that it stayed there. There it lives and there it reigns with all its allies: self-esteem, contempt of others, the desire to give orders to everyone and serve no one, pride in being Don Diego, and 'descended from the Goths,' showing off, excelling, boasting, much speaking, tall and hollow, gravity, pomp, daring with every kind of presumption, and all this from the noblest to the most plebeian."

—BALTASAR GRACIÁN, *El criticón*, seventeenth century

"If you ever feel like leaving moral Europe without even crossing the frontiers of geographical Europe, come to Spain. My God! They say that kings are passing away, but this is not true; here we have fifteen million kings at your service and at the service of everybody in general."

—DONOSO-CORTÉS, *Letter to Luis Veuillot*, nineteenth century

IT may be that pride is the key to the Spanish attitude toward society. The pride which allows the humble man to say, "I don't have the royal wish."

It is quite possible that this pride is, as Américo Castro thinks, an inherited Jewish or Arab characteristic. It is more possible that this tremendous pride of the Spanish people, which so impresses the foreigner—"Here everyone thinks he is a nobleman"—comes from the curious scale of values which sixteenth-century Spain devised for its descendants and which has easily lasted until today.

A very marked social scale provides each Spaniard with an inferior on whom he impresses his own authority and to whom he stands as chief. From the butler to the boy who cleans the shoes, from the cook to the kitchen boy, from the general to the private, there is always someone to order about in the same voice of gruff command that his own ears have heard, someone to satisfy the longing for power which we all bear within us. The most modest employee sees the shoeshine boy literally at his feet and bestows on him the benevolent sympathy of a client; how wonderful it is to look down on someone, to see him carry out his task with upward looks and pleasant smiles at one's jokes and from that position thank one for the generous tip—a generosity which is easily borne by an economy that has such wide differences of income as the Spanish one. And when we reach the bottom of the scale there remains the beggar to whom the soldier with his menial pay can give the tobacco which cost him little or the bit of bread they gave him for nothing. If this beggar has disappeared from many Spanish streets it has been due to the initiative of the authorities, keen on maintaining a perfect image of the town with an eye to foreigners, not because the Spaniard as such would wish to put an end to begging. Even today when a policeman arrests a poor man in a café, the murmur of the people shows the public's sympathy toward the arrested man and against the agent of authority. It is in vain for the latter to prove conclusively that the prisoner is a rascal

13

with no desire to work. In the first place, this accusation has no value in Spain. In the second, the existence of beggars to whom one can give is essential for the internal security of the Spaniard.

In saying this I am not denying the compassionate character of our people. But in this as in many other things the Spaniard reacts to what is visible and immediate, while he seems to ignore other things he is aware of but which are more remote. For example, in Catholic Spain there have been cases in recent years of frightful misery in convents, sometimes revealed in the press but quietly forgotten by those who could help relieve such conditions. For the cloistered nuns are not seen or heard in the streets, and the Spaniard's reactions are Polaroid: he is impressed one minute and then forgets what he has seen. It would never occur to a rich Spaniard, for instance, to send clothing or money to the unfortunate in Korea or India. For the Spaniard everything is instantaneous; there are few countries in which people think less about the future—in short, "What will be will be," "In a hundred years we'll all be bald," Don Juan's "There's a long time to go yet."

> *"What you give to the poor,*
> *God will repay you with interest."*

When we reach the beggar it looks as if we have come to the bottom. To whom can this man display his primacy? For one, to the same person from whom he receives the alms. This is a curious prerogative which comes from Arabic society, where the beggar is still accepted and recognized as a religious element—as one can see in the narrow streets of Tangiers or Casablanca. In receiving alms the poor Spaniard does a favor in his turn: he is putting the giver on the road to salvation, to heaven. For the believer it is almost a question of a contract —with the material advantages amply compensating the moral ones—which explains for many strangers the astonishing dignity with which the hand is held out and the unctuous reply which, when the obligation is avoided, contrives not to offend and postpones rather than denies: "It will be another day, brother."

Julio Camba comments: "Outside of Spain, there is really no begging. In order to beg it is necessary to play the violin, the ocarina or the accordion, sing ballads, dance or perform juggling tricks. Only Spain has made begging independent of the other arts and only the Spanish beggar reaches the public's heart without employing other Muses."

The fact is that this beggar is begging from millions of Spaniards who have lived and are living in the worst possible conditions, those who know bitter cold in bad houses, those who think it normal to have chilblains in winter and to sweat in torrents in summer because society has not given them the means to protect themselves against the fierceness of the weather, those who are still filling their stomachs with meals that lack nutritional balance; all these have lived for centuries with the illusion of possessing something which is inalienable and indestructible. It is race, a concept which in past centuries was, as we know, joined to a religious conviction. Yes, beneath the humblest of Spaniards, the poorest, the filthiest, there was still somebody. The Moors, the Jews.[1] "I have seven yards of Christian guts," cries the usually humble Sancho, using a phrase—*Cristiano viejo*, or old Christian—which implies a Christian descent without Jewish or Moorish blood. And Pedro Crespo reminds his son:

> By the grace of God, Juan
> you come of cleaner lineage
> than the sun, but not noble.

He reminds him of the first point so that he may aspire to everything. I honestly believe that race is at the root of the humblest Spaniard's conceit; the centuries have transformed the

---

[1] Although antisemitism in its European form hardly exists in Spain today, there does sometimes remain the age-old contempt for the child of Abraham. My brother Guillermo told me that in 1941, on the Portuguese frontier, a carabineer—unshaven, creased uniform, a cigarette stuck in his lips, with a badly dressed and worse-fed family—gave him a mocking wink as he inspected his passport: "Have you seen the cattle that's coming in the train? All Jews!" My brother went up to the sleeping car. It was the Rothschild family.

leaf without changing the root. When new tendencies and philosophies deprived race of its importance, the Spaniard pride of race became pride of nationality. The Spanish personality had been forged in the crucial sixteenth and seventeenth centuries, and the fact that the enemy disappeared from the land in the Jewish and Moorish expulsions ordered by the sovereigns did not change the concept of a people chosen by God.

Cadalso makes some interesting observations about Spanish pride:

> One of the defects of the Spanish nation in the opinion of other Europeans is pride. If this is the case, the proportion in which this vice is observed among the Spaniards is very strange, for it increases as the station of the subject decreases. The king washes the feet of twelve poor men on certain days in the year . . . with so much humility . . . that I . . . was filled with tenderness and burst into tears. The magnates and nobles of the highest rank, though they speak of their grandfathers from time to time, are on familiar terms with their humblest servants. The nobles of less elevated rank speak more often of their connections, relationships, intermarriages. The gentlemen of the towns are already rather heavy-going on the question of nobility. . . .
>
> All that has been said is little in comparison with the village hidalgo. He walks majestically in the sad square of his poor town, muffled in his bad cloak, contemplating the coat-of-arms above the door of his half-fallen house, giving thanks to God and to Providence for having made him Don So-and-so. He will not take off his hat (even if he could do so without unmuffling himself); he will not greet the stranger who arrives at the inn even if he is the general of the province or the president of its most important court. The most that he deigns to do is ask if the stranger is from an ancestral house known to the ancient Privileges of Castile, what coat-of-arms he has, and if he has relations who are known in these parts.

The difference in reaction is logical. Kings and high nobility can allow themselves the luxury of being affable to their inferiors and even religiously humble at times, because they are quite sure that their gesture will never enable the inferior to jump up to their level. Their confidence is easy precisely because the social situation is perfectly clear. As this security diminishes, misgivings increase and the pleasant gesture is stifled by a fear of provoking the confidence of the supposed inferior. The lower he is placed financially, the more precautions the nobleman takes to remind people of his only fortune, that of lineage. One remembers Don Quixote, easy always with Sancho but only up to a certain point, or the poor nobleman in Palacio Valdés' *José*.

The affectionate relationship between master and servant is always directly proportional to the social distance which separates them. That is why the gentleman who goes to a café in Spain talks familiarly to the waiter in a way that is not found in France or Italy; he is not afraid the man will finish up by sitting down beside him. (Something similar occurs in the South of the United States, where Negroes are treated as friends by the whites, much more affectionately than in the North, so long as they "keep their place.")

In a way, servants do not exist for visitors; that is, it never occurs to a Spaniard to introduce them to his guests. They are present physically but not socially.

Spanish pride maintains in force a caste system which has given way in other countries, where sooner or later there has been a revolution such as no Spaniard would accept—since, in acquiring other privileges, he would lose those he has had since infancy. He would agree to shortening the distance which separates him from the class above, but only if he were not asked at the same time to reduce that which separates him from the one below.

In the world of courtesy, Spain is a curious island in the sea of Romance Europe. The Portuguese, the French, the Italians, are infinitely more given to the affected and ceremonial phrase than the Spaniards, and keep up much longer the *vosse excelenza,* the *vous* and the *lei,* even among students of the university, where one would think it would have disappeared long before.

I have often wondered whether this is not another example of Spanish pride, which prevents a man from bending too much before a stranger—the same pride which made Lazarillo's squire watch the hands of an approaching acquaintance to see if he intended to take off his cap, so that he in his turn might reply to the salute and not be the first to offer it:

> One day he told me about his property and said it was in old Castile and that he had left his native place solely in order not to take off his cap to a gentleman who was his neighbor.
>
> "Please sir," said I, "if he was what you say he was and had more than you, were you not wrong not to greet him first, for you say that he greeted you too?"
>
> "He is and he has and he also greeted me but it would do him no harm to be the first some time."
>
> "I think, sir," I said, "that in such a case I would not feel this way, especially with those older and wealthier than I."
>
> "You are a boy," he answered, "and do not feel matters of honor, in which honest men have all their wealth nowadays. I tell you that I am, as you see, only a squire; but if I meet the count in the street and he does not take off his hat to me, the next time he is coming I shall go into a house pretending to have some business in it or go down another street if there is one before he arrives, so as not to greet him. For a nobleman owes nothing except to God and the King, and it is not right for an honest man not to have some respect for his person."

"It's not worth being a marquis if you don't know how."

The obsession with "gentlemanliness" affects any Spaniard, however modest, and to behave like a gentleman is something very important. Rinconete and Cortadillo, characters in Cervantes' "exemplary" novel, are a pair of lads in ragged clothing and are almost starving, but this does not prevent their greeting each other with such expressions as "Where are you going, *señor caballero*?"

But although the deeds do not fit the words, there remains in many Spaniards, even the most modest ones, the certainty that they have something more important than other mortals have, something above them: it is nobility, a series of qualities which may be summed up as physical and moral elegance, amiability to inferiors, and unbounded generosity. Not even the revolution, which from 1936 to 1939 imposed the use of "comrade" and "mate" in the most thickly populated regions of Spain, could remove halo and prestige from the title "señor"; knowing this, the Marxist propaganda hardly ever referred to the "señores" of Franco's Spain, but rather to the "señoritos," or young gentlemen. A young gentleman is naturally the son of a gentleman but this does not mean that he necessarily inherits the above-mentioned qualities. On the contrary, as he has had the name and the money since he was very young he can become a caricature of his father and let himself be dragged along by the easy life and by vice.

Economic circumstances have produced in Spain as throughout the world an alteration of modes of living, but underneath there persists a series of hierarchies. If a lady goes to the market and haggles too much, if she shows herself excessively tight with her money, if she mistrusts the vendor and humiliates her, the latter does not say "that lady," but "Get along with you: and they call themselves ladies!"—with which she shows she is maintaining the old respect and veneration for the ancient model which modern society tends to adulterate. And yet it is odd. The two most traditional institutions in Spain are the Church and the army, and they are perhaps the only ones which allow a man who does not possess financial means or social influence to reach the top. Many bishops come from humble peasant families, and many generals have risen from the ranks. But usually the tradition is maintained. We look at a bullfight poster. If there is a *rejoneador*, a mounted bullfighter, we find a "Don" before his name—Don Alvaro Domecq, Don Angel Peralta. The matadors who fight on foot are much richer, much better known, but their names are announced without a title. Why? Because the horseman is automatically a "señor," and the man on foot, in spite of having been the leading performer in bullfights since the eighteenth century, preserves a curious aura of humility which allows anyone to chuck him a cigar as a present when his performance has pleased the public. "Don Nobody is trying to be Don Somebody and Don Somebody is trying to be Don Somebody Important; no one is in his proper place."

In this business of trying to get as near as possible to the man above, we must remember the use of the familiar *tu*, which so surprises foreigners. This form of greeting was in the past confined to nobles with a long lineage, the grandees of Spain who, in using *tu* with one another, emphasized a brotherhood to which outsiders had no access. There sometimes occurred a case in which, when a man who had little right to do so put on his hat,[1] his fellows hastened to greet him as "Your Excellency" or "Your Grace," an apparently reverential form of address but actually of cutting coldness, meaning that he did not belong to the world which had received him—perforce—into its bosom.

With the Civil War came another revolution in custom. The extreme Left on one side and the Falange on the other, the comradeship of the trenches, where the whole range of the social classes met, set tradition at nought. When peace came and the normal life of society resumed, many who could have stayed this tendency received it gladly and encouraged it. Married ladies, however lofty their amorial bearings, found a wonderful coquetry in the new custom. It rejuvenated them. "Baroness, how are you (*usted*)?" became "How are you (*tu*), Adela?" Now boys of eighteen say "Hallo, man" to venerable

---

[1] The grandee had the right to put on his hat in the king's presence. The king, on raising a man to this station, would invite him, saying "Why do you not cover yourself, cousin?"—Tr.

elders who resign themselves to it from a holy fear of appearing out of date and therefore older than they really feel.

But if pride has changed the traditional customs of the upper class and of the aspiring middle class, it has not done so with the lower class. What is good manners in a duchess' drawing room is not so at a servants' ball, where the use of *usted* and *señorita* is obligatory when asking a girl to dance. The reason is obvious, for in this case the *tu* neither rejuvenates or modernizes. It recalls the way in which many Spaniards still treat their servants and is therefore a symbol of contempt, not of confidence among equals. The Spanish pride, which is relative but constant in all social classes, does not tolerate it. (In the same way the Spaniard of a higher class will introduce his wife as his *mujer*, a word which means both "wife" and "woman," while the workman, who has heard this expression applied to the washerwoman or the maid, will introduce his as his *señora*.)

In the old days the king was adored because he was in a way common property, and even today the ordinary Spaniard talks of the Duchess of Alba as everybody's heritage, in a certain way part of himself. He boasts of her name, her blood, her international prestige as if she were a member of his family. And he does the same with the bullfighter, the painter, or his national music.

Individual or collective pride, pride of a person or a people, ordinarily grows in proportion to material possessions. Spanish pride does not need this support, because it is an interior pride based as we have seen on a more intimate wealth, that of race (the great Spain of the Empire) or of religion (the *unique* religion, Catholicism). That is why the external manifestations of a Spaniard's pride have little in common with those of other people or other nations.

Thus the extraordinary in Spain is less extraordinary than in other countries, for it is not the result of an accumulation of wealth. The superfluous does not necessarily have to follow the necessary; if the superfluous is pretty, elegant or astonishing, it has a right of precedence over even the most urgent matters. While in a sensible country people first eat enough and afterward dress well, the Spaniard adorns himself first with the greatest elegance, even when his food leaves much to be desired, for nobody sees the latter.

The same principle is seen in architecture. Only in such ancient empires as Egypt and Assyria can we find someone like the king who built the palace-monastery of the Escorial; if it seems gigantic today, imagine what it was compared to the buildings of its day. The Escorial was not raised to house councils of the Indies, Castile, Aragon, Italy, which would have been logical, but for Philip II to offer to God as a sample of his devotion and pride.

The centuries have passed but the idea remains in force. After the Civil War, when half the people had no shelter, the Basilica of the Valley of the Fallen was begun; a mountain was excavated requiring an expenditure of men, money and material which would have sufficed to put a roof over the head of every Spaniard whom the fortunes of war had unhoused. While this was a project of the state, private enterprise was not left far behind. At a time when the houses of Madrid left much to be desired, what was for years the highest skyscraper in Europe was erected in the Plaza de España, and with the roads full of potholes the municipality started to dream of the most beautiful zoo in Europe.

It would be very easy to say that these are enterprises of a minority of politicians who act without counting on the approval of the people, but I do not believe that this is the case. The Spaniard is impressed by everything that is grand and magnificent even though it be useless or out of proportion to the country's means, perhaps because, being at home, he makes it his own, to serve as one more proof of his personal grandeur. The peasants of Philip II's Spain, half-dead with hunger, went into ecstasies at the Escorial, and I have heard many enemies of Franco make admiring and satisfied comments on the Basilica of the Valley of the Fallen, especially before foreigners: "You have nothing like it, have you?"

Famous sayings are usually famous because they reflect the soul of the people in a form which is concrete and easy to remember. When Unamuno reacted against accusations of inferior Spanish technology with "Let *them* (other countries) invent, then!" he was dismissing the importance of practical values. His exponents, cultured and sensitive men, made intrepid dialectical efforts to popularize this phrase which from every point of view is the most irrational that could be used by a man who asserts that he loves his people. But the fact remains that there is something Spanish in the heart of the most Cartesian of Unamuno's admirers which allows the phrase to give pleasure by its very effrontery, by its contempt for the normal elsewhere, by its pride, in short.

We find the same quality in the famous lines of *Las Mocedades del Cid* by Guillén de Castro:

> Always endeavor to attain
> what is honorable and important;
> but if you have made a mistake
> defend it and don't correct it.

Defend it and do not correct it, knowing that one is mistaken, knowing perfectly well that it is an error! In what mind is there room for this? In the one that values the heart more than the brain, the mind that does not dream of correction because it is humiliating—the Spanish mind, in short.

The grandiloquent phrase is, at times, a piece of impudence or a joke in which a reasoned petition is answered. When Ferdinand the Catholic asked Gonzalo de Córdoba for accounts of sums spent on the war, the other answered haughtily and sarcastically: "Picks, shovels and hoes, five million." Other paragraphs speak of perfumed gloves to resist the smell of enemies dead in battle, of new bells acquired because the old ones were broken in ringing so often for victory. All this was sonorous and bombastic, but naturally did not answer the king's question. On the contrary, it raised the suspicion that Don Gonzalo de Córdoba was offended at being asked for accounts, because he could not give them. Even if this had been true, his fame would have remained unblemished. The Spaniard will always be for de Córdoba in this historical legend. On one side is the king, suspicious, mistrustful, stingy, counting up his money; on the other a hero fighting and defeating the French, a hero whom the king obliged to descend from his glory to attend to this incredibly paltry matter. That's the way to answer, yes sir! And if he had kept something that was not his, what then? He deserved it a thousand times.

Morality, like religion, has no general force, but a particular one; it is a cloth that is applied to each man's measurements. The same action may be horrible today and splendid tomorrow, depending on who performs it; in the Spaniard's continual personalization, the quality of the man determines the gravity of the sin and not the other way around.

Take Calderón's description of the Spanish soldiers in *La rendicion de Breda*: "They suffer everything in the assault / But they will not suffer anyone to shout at them." The Spanish reader shivers with pleasure. "What guys they were!" He admires the Tercios of Flanders who destroyed without constructing, who produced more black legends than Antonio Pérez and the Inquisition put together. There is a romantic joy in picturing the rebel who kills, pillages and sacks out of pure Satanic pride. Catholic historians, without a word of protest or censure, describe the sack of Maastricht and the cries of "Spain, Spain! Kill, Kill!" That lofty type, the rebel, little subject to the laws of morality or religion, is still the Spanish hero par excellence. Any bandit is accepted if he has outstanding qualities, a good presence. Take Espronceda's Student of Salamanca, admired

> because on his very crimes,
> on his irreligion and arrogance
> Don Felix de Montemar
> placed a seal of grandeur.

And still today, after so much revolution and war, after so many social changes, Spaniards say admiringly of someone, "He's got class" or "He's got breeding."

Grandiloquent words sound well in Spanish ears: "Honor without ships is worth more than ships without honor"; "If you've no knife to kill my son, here's mine." Or, more recently,

"Empire, providential mission" on one side and "The people in arms," "The fatherland against the German-Italian invasion" on the other.

The grandiloquent phrase is like a banner beneath which the Spaniard likes to shelter, even if he does not exactly follow its meaning. It is interesting that here, instead of personalizing abstract concepts, the Spaniard remains absolutely independent of the very virtue he boasts of and very often does not let it interfere in the least with his private life.

Let us consider "honor," for example. Everyone likes to wrap himself in the folds of a fine-sounding, emphatic banner, recalling memories of glorious deeds. But living with it in accordance with its pure, strict meaning is another matter. Those representative Spaniards who appear in literature are all "men of honor" and are offended when anyone, at the sight of their frauds, tricks, hoaxes, blasphemies, or treacheries, doubts the fact. For them there is no contradiction between their public and private attitudes. They are gentlemen, so they are men of honor. And that is enough.

The noblest and best-respected of Spanish heroes, the Cid, tried to deceive some Jews by making them believe that the chests he left with them as surety for what they had lent him were full of gold and silver when in fact they only contained sand. This swindle seems perfectly natural to the author of the poem, who even forgets to tell us if the Cid at least paid the debt when he had become rich. "It's treachery, but it's mine!" cries Zorrilla's Don Juan, and when Don Luis, who has already been deceived twice, goes to his country house saying he trusts him, Don Juan answers grandly:

> No more than you may,
> and the better to show you
> my generous nobility
> tell me, Mejía, if I can still
> satisfy your honor.
> I won the wager from you honorably;
> but if it irks you so much,
> see if you can find some remedy
> and I will apply it to you.

Any Spaniard resents as a serious offense the fact that some-one doubts whether he is honorable, even if all the circumstances prove there is good reason for such doubt. A request to see a pass proving the right to enter a place is considered an annoy-ing imposition—"Do I look as if I would enter without the right?" An employee will cry out to high heaven if asked to sign in, showing he has arrived at the right time of the morn-ing—"I can't tolerate this lack of confidence! Who do they think they are?" And if he is informed, "Pardon, but you your-self have told me you generally arrive at the office at ten," he will give an angry reply: "And what's that got to do with it? I may arrive late at times but my father's son will not put up with people doubting him or watching him!" The discussion *should* end there.

The same thing applies to other qualities which a priori are considered innate in my countrymen—for instance, education and good manners, the gentlemanliness with which they all consider themselves to have been anointed since childhood. A Spaniard is automatically a gentleman. Once in a street in Madrid near the Gran Vía a girl who was walking in front of me was surrounded and besieged by a group of students who made the usual rude remarks (see Lust) while practically pre-venting her from moving. The girl looked at them scornfully and cried angrily, "Badly brought up!" When I heard this I imagined the boys would react by laughing at her expecting to find gentlemanliness in the street. I supposed that in a few phrases they would justify their preference for carnal violence, for violation and freedom of the passions in contrast to sophisti-cated and outdated manners. This, in the spirit of Espronceda's "Hurrah, cossacks of the desert, hurrah!" would at least have been logical. But I was amazed when the one who seemed to be the leader of the gang stiffened and said very seriously, "We're better brought up than you, gorgeous."

Is it that the Spaniard lives in two worlds, that the literary one forms his thinking by giving him an ideal model while the practical one marks his daily actions? Any relationship between the two would seem a mere coincidence.

In the same way as Spaniards have their suits made to

measure, so long as their finances allow, because appearance is the most important thing in their life, they create a religion for themselves to the measure of their personality. A direct relationship is established between God and the Spaniard, after which there is no need for theologians or bishops to clarify or explain a thing. The extreme of this spiritual position is represented by those mystics who find God in their own heart or feel absorbed by Him in direct communion without intermediary priests. The most difficult task for the Spanish Inquisition was to distinguish between authentic saints and those illuminated by doubtful moral taste, for they all had the same pretension—a direct line to the higher spheres.

This direct line is within the reach of any Spaniard, whatever his intellectual or moral category. "Do you imagine there is more than one God, one for me and another for you?"

Well, yes, in general this is what the Spaniard does believe. A God of his own to whom he can talk familiarly, ask favors from and make agreements with:

> I went up to high heaven,
> signed a contract with God
> that the day when you die
> I must die as well.

The Spaniard is wrapped up in religion from his cradle and applies its lofty theological concepts to pagan elements of his daily life. Another popular song runs,

> I love you more than God—
> see what a thing I've said!
> I deserve the Inquisition!

The last line is half in jest, half serious. His conscience reproaches him for a comparison which in another country would be sacrilegious. In Spain it is enough to cover oneself with an ironical remark:

> I should like to compare you—
> but no, I should be damning myself—
> with the Virgin of the Pilar:
> you're a tiny bit below her.

Reference is made to the high spheres of religion in justifying the human passions which are most important for the Spaniard. Bécquer, the finest of the Spanish romantic poets, whose popularity has survived the changes in literary fashions, has said:

> Today heaven and earth smile at me,
> Today the sun shines in the depths of my soul,
> Today I have seen her, I've seen her and she looked at me,
>   Today I believe in God!

And a spirit subordinating religion to love can hardly be restricted by the simple prohibition of the ministers of the Lord:

> The confessor tells me
> not to love you
> and I say, "Ay, Father,
> if you only saw her!"

"There's not a whore or a thief but has her or his devotion."

If any poor or uncultured person addresses God in the ways described, his confidence needs no greater moral authority. The Spanish prostitute wears religious medals even during her work, and the parish priest whose church is situated in a district of ill fame grows tired of seeing women praying to God for fortune to protect them before going their rounds. The incongruousness of this attitude led Richard Wright, the American Negro novelist, to call his book about our country *Pagan Spain*, but the adjective was wrong. It is not true that religious objects are amulets or fetishes without a real faith to sustain them. The prostitute's faith is much greater than that of other mortals because it is based not only on the mercy of God but on his comprehension. Be careful, however. This comprehension is not general; the prostitute does not believe that *all* those of her profession will be pardoned for their sins—not all of them, but she will be. Why she precisely? Because—and this is a reply I have often heard—God *knows* the reason for her behavior and that there is nothing for her to do but follow her road. A kind of contract has been made, then. While circumstances go on as they are, she will sin and God will assent, compassionate and comprehending. For her case is special, important and unique. "If I live well or badly," says La Celestina, "God is the witness of my reasons."

Every Spanish whore believes that her daily life is mixed up with such fabulous instances of the extraordinary that it could provide the substance for a literary narrative. Everyone who writes has heard it said with certainty "If I were to tell you my life, what a novel you could write!" This conviction on the part of a Spanish prostitute is based on pride, on two counts: her case is unique, and it must be so because only such amazing circumstances could explain her fall, rather as though she were a victim of cosmic forces.

Yes, the Spaniard looks at God face-to-face as an equal. The promises to which my compatriots are so given always have an air of give-and-take such as is granted only between equals: "You cure my daughter and I'll give you money for a hundred masses or go on my knees from such a place to such another." That most representative of Spaniards, Zorrilla's Don Juan Tenorio, *grants* heaven a chance to deal with him. The moment he decides to change his life, destiny ought to be ready to smile on him, protect him and accept him. When Don Gonzalo, naturally suspicious in view of the past, refuses to let him have his daughter and Don Luis mocks his humiliation, Don Juan dispatches them both with a quiet conscience, for as he then explains:

> I called to heaven and it did not hear me,
> and as it shuts its gates to me
> it is heaven, not I, that is responsible
> for what I do on earth.

Once a Spaniard has determined his place he does not consent to change it (see Sloth), even when whoever tries to do so has an obvious right. Already a part of Spanish folklore is the story of the Navarrese families which, when Pope Leo XIII proclaimed the bull *De rerum novarum*, reacted to that "leftist" declaration by praying every night "for the conversion of the Pope." During the last world war, a friend of mine heard a lady's indignant reaction to the news that fasting and abstinence had been suppressed as a temporary wartime measure. "Well, I shall go on fasting," she replied angrily. "If the Pope wants to damn himself, let him do so."

For every Spaniard has *his* Pope, an image which is already the original and not a copy. When what the Pope does fails to fit in with the personal idea we have of him, what is wrong is not the mirrored idea but the actual figure, *which ought not to be like that*. The phrase "more papist than the Pope" could be born only in Spain.

At bottom, perhaps because of the Spaniard's instinctive reaction against any command, devotion to the Pope has over the centuries been mixed with a certain pleasure in opposing him. The most Catholic historians relate without excessive anguish something so foreign to our religious tradition as the sack of Rome in 1527, when hundreds of priests were slaughtered by Spanish-commanded troops, or comment ironically on how the Pope finds it impossible to forbid bullfighting in Spain. And how amusing it is when the Cid throws down the French ambassador's chair and the Pope is frightened!

When the Spaniard goes to church he considers himself in his own house, not in God's. It seemed quite natural to the Catholic Spaniard of the Middle Ages, for example, that a good-looking woman should be sufficient to distract everyone, beginning with the officiant, as an anonymous poet has described:

> In Seville there's a chapel called St. Simon's where all the ladies go to say their prayers. My lady goes there too, the best of all . . . at the church door she shines out like the sun. The priest who's saying Mass cannot continue, the altar boys don't make the right responses, instead of "amen, amen" they say *amor, amor.*

And that old bawd La Celestina enters the church as if it were her office and the priests her clients:

When they saw me half a league away they would
leave the Book of Hours. One by one, two by two they
would come to where I was . . . each one to ask me
about his girl. Whichever man was saying Mass would
become confused when he saw me come in; he could
neither do nor say things right. . . .

In the seventeenth century it was natural that men and
women should observe each other and even flirt in the house of
God, among other reasons because it was the only place where
they *could* observe each other. An example from Lope de Vega
is one among many:

> You, madam, no longer remember
> that poor gentleman
> who the other day at church
> drank two fingers of water
> from the stoup, because you, madam,
> dipped in your finger
> and he said:
> Could a fountain in the Prado
> yield anything sweeter?

Seventeenth-century authors often situated romantic scenes
in the entrance of a church. Years later the moralists were still
complaining that the churches were "houses of conversation,"
and even today the Catholic foreigner is appalled at the familiarity with which people behave in the Lord's house, from the
greeting to the sweet exchange of looks. After all, the Spaniard finds any action in which he plays no part extremely
long. Nowhere in the world are there such short Masses as in
Spain, and if a Mass is still too lengthy the people are likely
to begin a stampede at the moment of the blessing, with the
noise of chairs and the shuffling of the congregation's feet a
compulsory accompaniment to the final prayers.

I am naturally speaking of those Spaniards who go to Mass.
For many the church is a place "as far as we go" on Sundays
and festivals of obligation, and in Spanish villages a typical
scene is that of the young men outside the church door waiting

for their wives and children inside. "The young man who listens to sermons," says a proverb mistrustfully, "has either no girl or no money."

Spanish men, I have often thought on observing the percentage who attend church, are more capable of dying in defense of a church door than of going through it. They like it to be there, it is a kind of metaphysical reserve for when they need it—there are few Spaniards who do not ask for a confessor when they feel they are nearing the end—but attendance is not in the proportion which would be logical in a country which has spent centuries killing and being killed in order that Flemings, Germans, American or Philippine Indians should embrace the only possible religion.

A great part of the Spaniard's misgivings with regard to religion comes from dislike of confession, a dislike which seems to be the greatest obstacle to being a good Catholic; confession is, above all, an act of humility which is completely at odds with our idiosyncrasy. This fact is not new. Already in the sixteenth century Malon de Chaide was complaining of the type who believes that his birth puts him above religious obligations:

> He kneels down like a crossbowman, blesses himself sloppily, so that you would not know if he were making a cross or a wiggle, and starts to let go and to cough up sins which make the walls of the confessional tremble; and if the confessor condemns them he comes out with a thousand coarse expressions and says that a man of his gifts does not have to live like a monk and it seems to him that everything is all right. And at the end he goes out as indifferent . . . as he came in and the wretched fellow is very pleased, as if God took into account that he descends from the Goths.

And finally, as witness to the familiarity with which Spaniards treat the church, is the poster which is still seen today: "You are requested not to spit, out of respect for the sacred place."

However Catholic he may be, the Spaniard always dislikes permitting another what he most appreciates, the intimacy of his home. Many violent and serious bedroom quarrels are due to the disgust with which the husband sees his conjugal life regulated, or at least advised, by his wife's confessor.[1] This kind of thinking is probably the greatest obstacle to his wholehearted acceptance of a religion which otherwise offers many advantages, principally a good chance of being saved. "A little contrition gives the soul salvation," says the Spaniard, taking the phrase as a blank check which may be filled in at any moment with the date of death and a certain negotiation of sins. The end is always distant.

"There's a long way to go yet!"

Tirso's Don Juan said this to someone who was warning him that "There is God and there is death." Obviously there is death, but there is also plenty of time. How much? Just as much as is convenient, for the Spaniard always adapts the laws to his personality and never the other way around. And with such a view, the Spaniard's private Catholicism allows him complete liberty in life, always counting on God's charity and His capacity for pardon. To give himself more security, the Spaniard has exalted the figure of the Virgin as mediator between the sinner and his judge, a kind of advocate who at the last moment intercedes in the same way as is done in the ministries: "Do what you can for this gentleman, for although he may be in the wrong he's a great friend of mine."

In the medieval poet Gonzalo de Berceo's "Milagros de nuestra Señora," a clergyman who is lost and drunk but who has always found time in his dissipation to pray to the Virgin is saved by her from the devil in the form of a lion, so that he may have time for repentance. In the nineteenth century Zorrilla gave us the legend of Margarita la Tornera, a nun who, consumed by an insane love for a Don Juan, prays to the Virgin

---

[1] From this, the extreme suspicion of the psychiatrist follows logically. Spanish specialists in this branch of medicine bewail the difficulties they run into with the average Spaniard. "I don't tell my affairs to a priest, why should I tell them to you!"

and begs her pardon preparatory to leaving the convent. When she is abandoned by her lover and returns repentant to the convent, she finds her place occupied by a girl looking exactly like herself. The Virgin has taken her place so that no one should be aware of the sinner's absence.

The Spaniard also likes religion because it represents a guarantee of his good name—that is, as it applies to his wives, sisters and daughters. Many Spaniards who only attend church to perform a duty are pleased to see the women of the family going to the tribunal of the confessional and to Communion, for they know by experience that her fear of later having to confess her sin is the best control on the Spanish woman's temperament. It is also the best barrier against temptation, and getting over this barrier is part of the emotion of a conquest—so much so that without it the thing loses attractiveness. As a Spaniard said when he saw the religious indifference of a Swedish girl with regard to the sexual act, "The truth is that if she is not damned I don't enjoy myself."

And then there is, connected with pride, religious exhibitionism. Such processions as those during Holy Week in various Spanish towns would not be possible except as demonstrations of the power and wealth of those who take part in them. "You ought to see how we carry 'our' Virgin, 'our' Christ!" It is clearly always a question of something of one's own: our statue is always better and produces more miracles than that one. To explain to a foreigner just why the Macarena is more beautiful and more miraculous than the Virgin of the Seven Sorrows is a really difficult task—we have to appeal to vague references, to the tradition and originality of our people.

In a certain seventeenth-century memoir, the chief character tells how his defeated enemy pleaded, "Do not kill me, for the sake of the Virgin of the Carmen." And the hero replied, "You've been lucky . . . you named *my* Virgin and that has saved you. If you'd appealed to another one you would not get away alive."

Up to the eighteenth century there were penitents in the Spanish processions who beat their backs rhythmically with a

wax ball at the end of a cord, the ball imbedded with pins and
pieces of glass which tore the flesh. Officially this was done from
the Christian's desire to suffer for the Lord, as He had suffered
for us. But travelers and natives who wrote about it noticed
that the presumed torture was an exhibition of virility, made
more manifest by the care the flagellants took that the ladies of
their thoughts should see their performance from close up and
should even be splashed with the generous blood of their hero.

The second commandment, "Thou shalt not take the name
of God in vain," seems completely useless to the Spanish
Catholic, who hardly ever employs God's name in any other
way. *Dios mío* is more often used when the forward's shot at
the goal has missed than to beseech divine aid at an agonizing
moment. *Dios lo quiera* (may it please God) is used both for
worthy and unworthy things and in reality is one more catch-
word like *Vaya con Dios* (go with God), *Dios te ayude* (God
help you), *Dios te proteja* (God protect you). They are nearly
all an inheritance from Moslem customs and some have come
down with the same sound. *Ojalá* (equivalent to "I only wish
that . . ."), for instance, is simply *Aj-Ala* or "would to God!"
in Arabic. *Ole*, which is used at the bullfights when the pass has
been good, is another invocation similar to *wa-allá*, "Oh God!"

But the habit of church goes further, and Spaniards use the
nomenclature of religion for the most profane situations. For
instance, one of the passes at a bullfight is called a Veronica;
the origin of the name is that the capes, extended in front of
the bull's head, reminded someone of the moment when
Veronica lovingly wiped the sweating, bleeding face of the
Savior with her cloth, and the holy face remained imprinted on
the towel. It seems altogether normal to the most Catholic of
Spaniards to mention the two or three veronicas, culminating
in a half-veronica, that so-and-so gave to the third bull of the
afternoon.

The proverbs used by Spaniards are continuous examples of
this religious impregnation which makes them keep on mentioning sacred things without the least intention of committing
a heresy (even the priests use many of these proverbs).

When a man dresses in a way that does not conform to the aesthetics of his social position, it makes him look "like a Christ with pistols"; absolute confidence in someone is ridiculed ironically with "trust the Virgin and don't run"; the relationship between two persons of doubtful moral character is explained by "God creates them and they come together." "May God catch us when we've confessed" began as a sensitive prayer that death might overtake the Spaniard in purity of soul; today it is applied to the possibility of not being prepared for any event. A difficulty is defined by "There's no God to settle that one"; of a man who is lucky it is said that "he spoke to God"; a faraway place is situated "where Christ cried three times." There are those who, when they are in a tight spot, look sadly up to heaven and cry "Come down, Manolo!", using the familiar diminutive for Emmanuel.

Other examples cannot be construed as definite, clear irreverence. Before a wooden statue of a saint a man may say, "Are you trying to lord it over me, who knew you when you were a cherry tree?" and await the divine gift without moving from the spot, without doing anything to approach Him. "If God wants to be good to me He knows where to find me."

This familiarity with the deity is so deeply rooted that the triumph of the Right in the Spanish Civil War has not been able to change it, though it has led to the prohibition of any magazine or publication that attacks the principles of the Catholic Church, makes fun of its ministers or its worship, or presents them in an unpleasant light. For twenty-five years, the regime forbade the publication of any work included on the Index of Prohibited Books in Rome. (This ban was recently lifted.)

Nevertheless, during all this time, every year at the end of October and beginning of November the Spaniards mass to see Zorrilla's *Don Juan Tenorio*, a play whose leading character reminds us from the first of his irreverence:

> I escaladed the cloisters
> I heeded not what was sacred,

> audaciously I respected
> neither occasion nor place;
> nor have I stopped to distinguish
> between the cleric and layman.

Furthermore, Don Luis boasts of having robbed a bishop's treasury and shot the provincial head of the Order of St. Jerome.

But these are still only boasts. Soon there come actual deeds. Don Juan assaults the convent and kidnaps a novice who was about to profess. The abbess is made fun of and on top of that has to hear herself insulted by the father of the girl: "Where are you going, Commander?" she asks. "Imbecile, after my honor that was stolen from you right here!"

This might still be considered unextraordinary in officially Catholic Spain if at the end Juan received his desserts in the form of eternal damnation. But no, the public loves him too much, he is too sympathetic a character for this to happen. While Tirso's Don Juan, like Molière's, goes to hell as a punishment for his scandalous life (though Tirso's character has kidnapped no novice), Zorrilla's is saved through the intercession of his beloved. The author himself realized that this ending was a little strange, theologically speaking, and makes Doña Inés explain:

> I have given my soul for you
> and God grants you your doubtful salvation
> for my sake.
> A mystery this which a creature
> is too puny to understand;
> only in a life that is purer
> will the just come to comprehend
> it was love that saved Don Juan
> on the brink of the grave.

The audience comes out of the theater very optimistic. Their idea that there is always time to repent has been confirmed.

If a somewhat sophisticated Spaniard is asked about *Hermana San Sulpicio*, he smiles contemptuously. "It's a rose-colored novel, my fifteen-year-old sister is reading it." Since it was published it has been considered a novel which may be put into the hands of any little girl who attends a religious school. It is, however, the story of a nun—not a novice, this time—who falls in love with a gentleman. Sister San Sulpicio—so gay that she even dances *Sevillanas* in her habit—lets herself be persuaded by the Galician Ceferino Sanjurjo, and against the wishes of the Church and of her mother returns to secular life and ends up marrying him. Among other characters in the book is a wicked, selfish priest.

The author of the work, Armando Palacio Valdés, is considered a writer of the Right, or at least conservative. His book implies no thesis against the Spanish Church. It is simply one more example of the bold way in which religious subjects are treated by most Spaniards.

The certainty about the "direct line" to which I have referred produces in many Spaniards the sensation that they are carrying on a particular, private conversation with God, that the Lord will drop everything to attend to them. This way of thinking gave birth to a little story I was told in Madrid and which I sincerely believe would be impossible in another country: An elegant gentleman stands before the Christ of Medinaceli, a much-venerated statue, along with a badly dressed and hungry-looking poor man. They are both visibly worried, obsessed with their own necessities, and without noticing each other they pray aloud. The rich man implores the Lord's aid for the bank to guarantee him the five million he needs to back up a deal in which he sees great possible profits. The poor man asks with the same confidence and faith for five hundred pesetas, which will enable him to pay the landlord so that he will not be thrown out of his house. The prayers become threaded together, they mingle in the air; both men have their eyes fixed on the statue:

"Lord, it doesn't cost you anything, let them guarantee those millions. . . ."

"Those pesetas, Lord, so I won't find myself in the street . . ."

"All my commercial life depends on this, Lord, don't let me fall into disgrace, into bankruptcy. . . ."

"Lord, it's extremely cold, don't let them chuck me out. Grant me this money. . . ."

"Lord, five million . . ."

"Lord, five hundred pesetas . . ."

They are both almost shouting. Suddenly the elegant man pauses in his prayers, hastily opens his wallet and pulls out a five-hundred-peseta note.

"Take this," he says to the poor man. "Don't distract His attention from me!"

The contract, the arrangement *Do ut des*, "I give to receive," naturally can lead to the feeling of having been "done" at times. In several Spanish villages a procession is remembered in which the holy Patron was solemnly brought out in order to aid the people in imploring rain. After hours had been spent under the sun without a cloud's appearing, the saint was hurled into the river by the indignant multitude.

The union of Church and state brought about by the Empire solved, once and for all for many Spaniards, the problem of religion, which *must* be the Catholic one. Conversion to Protestantism is as rare in Spain as is conversion to Christianity among the Arab peoples (every missionary in Morocco speaks of his failure in this sense), for the Catholic religion has been a part of Spanish life for so many years that it is like a second skin which may be torn off but not replaced. The Spaniard lives as a Catholic even when he is a revolutionary.

"We always go after the priests, with a candle or with a stick," said Agustín de Foxá. The destruction of churches and the killing of clergy in republican Spain were seen by some observers as a desperate attempt to put an end to an atmosphere which surrounded and oppressed the most anticlerical of revolutionaries. And who can doubt that the blasphemer, and there are heaps of them in Spain with twisted and baroque ways of expressing themselves, is a believer at heart? How can one offer gross insults to something that does not exist? Chesterton recommended that those who believed this possible should try to blaspheme, for example, the god Thor.

The Spaniard defends the Catholic religion because it is his, and being his it must be perfect. There is a revealing anecdote about a bootblack of Cadiz who made mocking remarks about a priest who was passing by—much to the joy of the client, a Protestant bishop traveling incognito in Spain. Becoming enthusiastic about the evangelical possibilities, the foreigner began to explain to the bootblack the differences of his own belief, the greater respect it held for the human conscience, the political liberty, the permission—so natural—for clergymen to marry. He was in full flood when he was interrupted by the bootblack.

"Don't tire yourself, mister. I don't believe in my own religion, which is the true one, so how am I going to believe in yours?"

Is this just a joke, a boast by a man of the people who did not know how to answer? Here is what a famous, cultured Spaniard said in a parliamentary speech in 1869: "I, gentlemen, do not belong to the world of theology and faith: I belong, I believe I belong, to the world of philosophy and reason. But if I ever had to return to the world which I left, I should certainly not embrace the Protestant religion. . . . I should return to the beautiful altar which inspired me with the greatest feelings of my life: I should return to prostrate myself on my knees before the Holy Virgin. . . ." At heart, the same sentiment as the Cadiz bootblack's, said more eloquently (the speaker was the famous parliamentarian Emilio Castelar).

The Spaniard makes religion his own to such an extent that although it should be universal, being Catholic, he has it serve regional interests. Witness the waiter who, when a stranger expressed doubt while watching the float of "The Judgment of Pilate" as to who a certain figure was (Pilate's wife advising her husband), answered, "That one? That's the one who very nearly left us without Holy Week!" For the good Sevillian, two thousand years of Christianity have existed only to ensure that the city on the Guadalquivir may celebrate its beautiful festival.

Besides, it is important for the Spaniard to remain Catholic because it is obvious that his nationality gives him a head start toward heaven. How is God going to use the same strict rules for a Dutchman as for a Spaniard, someone from the land of the Virgin of the Pilar?

Pride is, I believe, the sin from which the Spanish saint finds it most difficult to free himself. St. Teresa accuses herself of vanity in her autobiography, for the very fact of telling her life, even though by order of her confessor, evidently implies a certain self-esteem.

And what pride could be greater than that of the authentic Tenorio, Juan de Mañara? He thought he was serving an exquisite example of humility by casting himself from his height, from the vanity of "everything is permitted to me" to the abyss of penitence: "I am nothing, let everyone tread on my body when entering the Hospital of Charity in Seville." His memorial tablet reads: "Here lies the greatest sinner in the world."

Could anything be more insolent?

This pride may be supported by a general concept—that of race—without losing its principal individual character. The Spaniard does not mean "we," but "I." The "old Christian" with no Jewish or Moorish blood, or the Spaniard who lives on past glories—"You should see what we did in America" or "when we won at Lepanto"—is always thinking of himself, of the rights which this heritage has given to *him*, of the position, unattainable to others, which this history confers on *him*. This is why he chooses from the past, or even from the present, what suits his ego, unconsciously rejecting that which might damage the image he likes to create of himself. *Arrogante*, offensive in its equivalents in other languages, is a word of praise in Spanish.

If the Spaniard is so touchy about national self-criticism as to resent adverse comments by foreigners, it is because he does not feel absolute solidarity with anyone, Spanish or foreign. I believe this is the most logical explanation as to why normally sensitive people do not feel the least disgust or remorse today for the crimes committed in the Civil War. In the first place, no one accepts any responsibility for the horrors of the other side; it is as if they had been committed by people from another planet. Those were the enemy, capable of anything! But were they not Spaniards too? The reply might be something like "If they were, they didn't deserve to be!" We shall see throughout this book how easy it is for the Spaniard to get rid of the Gordian knots which he finds in dialectic. Just by cutting them.

But the fact is that this individualism goes further than simply choosing sides. Those on his own side are also strangers at the moment of truth, and this is not a question of avoiding responsibility, as it might be in other countries. When the Spaniard retires into his shell, he admits neither brothers nor coreligionists. When he is confronted with a reality—"in such a village your side did this and that"—he shrugs his shoulders: "Ah well, they must have been mad." They are "others," they are apart, it is nothing to do with him.

The Spaniard lives *with* a society, never within it. His personality is covered with prickles which stand up dangerously at any attempt to make him collaborate in some enterprise. He is unsuited to what in science is called teamwork, and this lack has been often recognized as a determining factor in the slowness of Spanish scientific progress. Our geniuses, for example, are exceptional in the sense of being unique, and rarely come from any particular school.

In the Spaniard, says Américo Castro, "the direction of vital dynamism goes from the object to the person, for this is the reality of his own makeup." This is true to such an extent that he appropriates to himself all that touches him from near or far. The Spaniard, when speaking of his day's work, says, "I had *my* breakfast, I read *my* paper, I lit *my* cigarette, I got into *my* bus"—but curiously enough changes when referring to "the office" (see Sloth).

The Spaniard feels in general an instinctive reluctance to join associations. Civil wars and the fate of those who fought in several of them have not exactly helped change this attitude. Compare the number of societies in Spain with the number in England or in the United States, for example, where it is normal for a citizen to be a member of five or six different organizations—patriotic, charitable, religious or recreational. When the Spaniard joins a club, he does not usually think of collaborating with others to solve problems, but of finding a comfortable place where he can tell others what he thinks of the world in general, and of the Sánchez family in particular.

That is why the organization to which he cannot help

belonging, the state, is viewed with suspicion. The state is a hated entity which is never seen as the necessary link between the individual and society but rather as a conglomeration of ambitions which is trying to regulate the life of Juan Español, without having the least idea of that life and with the simple purpose of abusing it. The nature of the state has no importance in this regard. It is all the same if it is a republic, a monarchy, or a dictatorship. It is always a prying enemy of life, which must be dealt with by paying it the least possible attention. The laws which the state decrees have some value while the ink is still wet, before a few months have passed. On hearing of a man's unethical scheme, I have sometimes asked why there is no law forbidding it. It has not been spoken of for a long time, comes the answer. For us, silence is equivalent to abolition. In Spanish Colonial America the holder of an *encomienda*, a feudal fief, showed his respect for the king who had sent an order incompatible with his own opinion by putting the decree on his head and pronouncing solemnly—without irony—"It is respected but it is not obeyed."

Every Spaniard feels authorized to deceive the state by trying to evade the payment of taxes. We have to go a long way up the moral scale of Spaniards before finding one who would equate cheating the tax collector with assuming possession of someone else's money. Many people incapable of keeping ten pesetas that belong to an unknown person will not hesitate to trick the state out of thousands and thousands. Many who would regard the first action with horror will smile admiringly on the second. The first is stealing, the second is being smart. For after all, "Who robs a thief?"

"What is in Spain belongs to the Spaniards"

This is why smuggling is so widely accepted in Spain and considered a normal activity even among the most religious of Spaniards, the Basques. A character in Pérez Galdós' novel *Fortunata y Jacinta* puts it thus: "For him, Estupiñá, what the treasury calls its own belongs not to it but to the nation, that is to say, to Juan Particular, and to trick the treasury is to return to Juan Particular what is his."

Furthermore, this contempt for the property of the state is extended to any great organization which, perhaps just because it is great and therefore *dehumanized*, need not be respected. We all have friends who collect ashtrays from hotels and restaurants or who take mementos from the big stores as if they were doing a kindness. I have often asked where the limit is, that is to say when stealing begins to be stealing, at what price; and men have looked at me as if I were crazy. For them it is perfectly clear. It depends on the size (something small is always suitable) and on the place (never in a private house). A unique morality, which in other respects is more universal. Take books, for example. It seems quite natural to the most honest of Spaniards to keep a friend's book for years. Technically he continues to consider it as borrowed, his conscience tranquil, but his intention of returning it in the days that are left of his life is nonexistent. And he who lends it does so aware in a certain way of the tremendous risk he is running, but with a very Spanish eagerness to be able to comment on something which they will both then know.

Once, it was a Saturday, I took a book from the house of the humorist Tono. It was short and I had nothing to do during the weekend, so that by Monday morning I had finished it and sent it back to him by a bellboy. At midday he rang me up: "What's the matter? Are you angry?"

This was the only logical explanation that had occurred to him for my unheard-of behavior.

And how is it when the Spaniard forms part of the state? Ortega y Gasset tells us with his usual perspicacity:

> We notice at once that the Spaniard in his job feels as if he were in an orthopedic apparatus. We should say that his job hurts him continually, for his personal life carries over without sufficient inhibition, and as it does not coincide with official conduct it runs up against it. We see that in every situation the man feels a horrible longing to do something different from what the regula-

tions prescribe. It is moving to imagine the suffering of
a traffic policeman in Madrid because he is not allowed
to suspend the normal order of the service to let a nice
girl pass.

But how then are we to explain the minimal number of
organizations and public services that *do* exist, particularly if
we add the sloth of the average Spaniard to his basic lack of
interest? The answer is that when collective interest fails he
maintains his personal pride. When a Spanish employee furi-
ously questions someone who seems to him to be trying to enter,
without paying, the hall he is protecting, when a tramway
inspector triumphantly discovers in the crowd of passengers
someone who was absentminded when the moment to hand
over his ticket arrived, he is hardly ever moved by duty but by
his personal prestige; he is quite carefree about the interests of
the state or the tramway company, but no one is going to pull
his leg or make a fool of him. The fight is not between an
abstract entity and an individual but between two individuals,
between two human beings.

The state, in general, is the enemy. This is why, when the
espontaneo (a young man who jumps into the ring and tries to
go at the bull) is led off by the police, the crowd takes advantage of its anonymity to boo the public forces and applaud the
boy who has been trying to break the law.

This aversion to authority only applies, however, when one is
safe. A Spaniard has only to be provoked by someone—it takes
very little for him to feel provoked—for the appeal to public
order to be immediate and urgent: "Look out, police! Send for
a policeman; they must arrest the man!" Any small incident in
a theater, something which in another country would be solved
by the friendly intercession of a third party, in Spain produces
shouts from all sides. "To prison, take him to prison." It often
happens that the shouter does not know what it is all about,
but that does not matter. He has been upset, his relaxation, his
amusement have been interrupted. To prison with the scoun-
drel. Dungeon, fetters, bread and water. "Who the hell does he
think he is, man?"

But in principle, all legal ordering of life appears to the Spaniard as an intrusion on his rights, which he does not mention in the plural but in the singular. "There is no right!" he cries when something injures him, that is to say, there is no law (*derecho* means both "right" and "law"). Upon his being harmed, all the legal ordering of the country has been annulled.

It is enough to watch a Spanish citizen driving a car through the streets to be sure of the censure with which he regards any attempt to restrain his sacred liberty to pass on the right or the left, to stop to talk to a friend or to watch a young lady cross over. Habit does not soften this reaction, and the taxi drivers, who ought to be accustomed to the prohibitions of the traffic laws, are the ones who make the most merciless demonstrations against them. There are drivers who make infinite detours through narrow and inadequate side streets only to avoid the traffic lights and not, as some suspicious passengers may think, to lengthen the journey. If you pay by the hour it will be the same thing. And when he comes up against a red light, a driver's patience squeaks as violently as do the brakes. The light seems a personal offense, something which society is doing to him, Jesús Fernández, to injure him, to humiliate him, to torment him. "Let's go! Let's see if we stay here all day!" As soon as the amber light appears he shoots off toward the next street to repeat the same agonized monologue.

The idea predominating is that each man's intelligence is superior to anonymous regulations. The lights and the police— I have often heard—do nothing but complicate things. It's all very well for square-headed people like the Germans, but we— well, if all the lights were removed at once the traffic would move much better.

The irritation of the Spaniard at everything that gets in his way is not confined to men or their institutions. It extends to nature as well. You should hear, for instance, the way Spaniards react verbally to heat and cold as soon as they pass the point they consider perfect for their organism: "No one can put up with this! What a day! Just look at it!" They wipe away the sweat with a gesture of rage, curse the water that falls from the sky. Surprised by this attitude, foreigners have asked me whether it is a question of a temperature unknown until then in the country, something like an unexpected plague. When I tell them it is not, that this is the normal climate for the season, they are astounded. But why are they complaining, then? Aren't they used to it? Doesn't the same thing happen to everyone?

No, I reply, the Spaniard never gets used to discomfort, and the fact of being one among millions who are suffering at this moment gives him absolutely no consolation. On the contrary, he sees himself as the only individual whom Nature, for no reason, is punishing in a way that is so disagreeable (and humiliating, for he cannot avenge himself on her).

I remember a scene many years ago in the Plaza de Manuel Becerra, today de Roma, in Madrid. I was first in a line for a trolley-bus. When I was already on the bus platform and ready to pay the conductor for my ticket, a boy of about nine passed almost between my legs. His mother, behind me, had pushed him forward as a *commando* to look for a place. When I entered he was sitting down with his arms and legs spread out to cover more space, and he looked at me with as much defiance ("Just dare to take it from me!") as fear ("He's bigger than me and maybe he'll chuck me out"). Of course, the one thing there was no trace of in his expression was respect for the rights of others, but that was not his fault. His parents, his elder brothers, his uncles, had presented society to him as a jungle in which nothing can be achieved if one does not think first of oneself and after that of nobody.

That child, now grown up, is probably applying to traffic, to business, to his daily treatment of his fellows, the same theory which shot him like a bullet between the passengers' legs to wrest their precedence from them. His mother had surely described it later at home: "If it hadn't been for him I shouldn't have got a seat, but he's so smart. . . ."

In politics, the individual's sense of certainty has led logically to a plethora of candidates for leading posts which in other countries would be considered the private preserves of those who have devoted care and study to public administration. The history of the Spanish *pronunciamientos* is clear proof that the command of a regiment or division automatically makes one feel equally capable of governing a country. At bottom the general who leads a rising does no more than put into practice— because he has the means to do so—the dream of most Spaniards: to govern, not for the sake of his subjects' happiness but to satisfy an ambition of his own, not so much to rule as not to be ruled, not so much to guide as to not have another guide him.

Another curious thing about the general who leads a rising is that he considers it incredible that another officer should attempt the same thing against the new authority. In 1844 Narvaez wrote to General Zurbano, who was threatening a new *pronunciamiento*: "By violating the law, as I once violated it, you are moving straight towards a bottomless pit." And he threatened to shoot him.

It is not by chance that the individualist is more prevalent in Spain than the organizer. Spain does not produce Napoleons or Alexanders, but she has produced Indibil, Mandonio, Cortés, Pizarro, Cabrera, Viriato, Daoiz, and Velarde. Large-scale war presupposes a meeting of wills which is repugnant to the Spanish character. The Spanish warrior prefers to be a guerrilla fighter, in the small war involving the least possible number of men, under leaders who often fight among themselves, for all their common aims. One rung lower we have the "generous" bandit whose cruelty the common people forget in order to rejoice in his independence and his challenge to society and especially to the government. The legend of the man who robs the rich to help the poor was perhaps born, subconsciously, to legitimize admiration for the outlaw.

When people speak of Spain's being a romantic country, I imagine they are thinking of her characteristic features as found in her literature, features invoking the principles of romanticism: the admiration for the rebel (Don Juan is, above all, a rebel), for the pirate, the pitiless soldier of the Tercios of Flanders, the prostitute who leaves a society because it is unjust; the praise of whoever lets himself be moved by passion rather than reason, by the heart rather than the brain; the seeing in religion not a series of laws to follow but a beauty with an aesthetic attraction on one side and a dramatic conflict (salvation/damnation) on the other; the cult of death penetrating the Hispanic soul; and so on.

In the national rising of 1808 against the French, the fact that juntas arose in every region can be explained by the Spanish need to act autonomously. But it is more difficult to understand —for anyone who is not a Spaniard—why each junta must be not only separate but supreme, first.

Years ago I had occasion to serve in a military office to which many recruits reported. To avoid congestion and make the job easier, we had formed branch offices of sorts, to which we sent the lads once they had been organized into groups. I would call to fifteen or twenty of them, appoint one of them their leader, and finish by saying, "Now you will all go with this gentleman I've appointed to register. You may go now."

The march would begin. And always, always, there would remain one with a mocking smile for the group, for the "flock."

"But you—didn't you hear you were *all* to go?"

"Ah," he would say. "*Me* as well?"

Why "he" was not included in "all of you" can only be understood in Spain.

Even in something as clamorous and collective as the crowd at a bullfight, we find the superindividualist. When the bullfighter is making a circuit of the ring, returning garments and smilingly thanking the people for their applause, there is usually one spectator in each section who stands up with the others and moves his forefinger from side to side while he repeats gloomily, "No, se-ñor!" He then looks at the rest with a satisfied air, sure of himself. *He* has not been deceived by the *faena* designed for the masses; *he* knows very well what is *torear* and what is not *torear*. In short, he is enchantingly alone.

In dancing, in singing, the tendency to individualism grows as we move from north to south. Above La Mancha the people normally sing in chorus and dance in groups, the Galician *la muñeira*, the Catalan *sardana*, the Basque *zorcico*. But south of Despeñaperros, singing is individual and so is dancing. Even in the *Sevillanas* danced by groups, each girl lifts her arms and moves her feet in her own personal way, and the dancers would probably be annoyed if someone told them that the movements of the group were all the same, that you could not distinguish one from another. It will be said that the northerners are just as Spanish as the southerners. This is true, but the "Spanish" dance that is par excellence the most characteristic one, with the possible exception of the Aragonese jota, is Andalusian; there must be some reason for this.

But there is one organization which, if it is to survive, needs to break this code of individual license. That is the army, which could simply never form battalions or regiments of independent Spaniards if it trusted only to them. To counteract this centrifugal tendency, so contrary to what is required of an armed force, the discipline of our army has been one of the strictest in the world, including the Germans under the Kaiser and Hitler. It must be remembered in this statement that the ordinary German has a spiritual and collective discipline in his daily life which makes him adopt *any* regulation as the sacred book which guides his footsteps. For the German, the heel-clicking, the standing to attention before a sergeant, means no more than a slightly increased emphasis on an obedience to which he has been conditioned since childhood. For a Spaniard accustomed to sprawling on benches and leaning against walls, to be rigid, motionless and *not talking* is a psychological shock he remembers all his life. If we note a certain respectful stiffness in a peasant or a workman we are addressing, we may be assured that it was acquired in military service.

A Spaniard may be above society or outside it, but he never collaborates with it. Aside from the old superstitious respect for the king, who was "above everybody," many Spaniards have felt uncomfortable when being only one part of something collective. This is why simple army officers—Espartero, O'Donnell, Serrano, and Prim in the last century; Primo de Rivera, Sanjurjo, Mola, and Franco in this one—assumed the personal right to stand above the masses, and often succeeded.

For the same reason many Spaniards who did not have political or financial means for command chose not to obey and declared war on the whole existing social organization. These were the anarchists. It is not by coincidence—no coincidence lasts so long—that Spain has had the most active anarchist groups in the world, responsible for killing three prime ministers, wounding another, and making attacks on the king twice in twenty-five years. The Italian anarchists distinguished themselves individually but never succeeded in dominating a single city. In Spain, it is calculated that two million anarchists' votes (Spain had only twenty-five million inhabitants then) gave victory to the Popular Front in 1936. I was living in a Catalan village with an anarchist regime in the first weeks of the Civil War and saw the establishment of its systems at close range. Abolition of money, barter of products, burning of churches, free love—the anarchist is the extreme consequence of Spanish pride: he rejects God, the state and society, all entities which eulogize collective norms of behavior. Anarchism in Spain has converted itself into a political organization with rules and programs, but I am convinced that what led thousands of Spaniards to join it was the dream of most of the inhabitants of the peninsula: to do what they really felt like doing.

When a Spaniard joins with others to form a political party, he does no more than enlarge his personal ego according to the circumstances, and so the party is as vociferous and loath to compromise as each of its components; the rules of the political game—if some win, others lose—which are supposed to be accepted by all those who take part in it, are generally despised. Before the elections of February 1936, the leader of the Spanish Socialist Party, the leader of the National Monarchist Block, the leader of the Communist Party, and the Anarchists all stated publicly that they would only respect the result of the elections if they should win but never—loud applause—if they should lose.[1] The incongruence of this declaration with what was officially called an electoral campaign occurred to no one, not

[1] The anarchists were truer to individualism in the previous elections when they shouted "Workers, do not vote! The vote is the denial of personality!"

even to enemies. The rising of the Left in October 1934 was
the consequence of having lost the election in 1933. The rising
of the Right in 1936 was due to its having been defeated in the
voting some months before.

Only to pride, to the gigantic Hispanic pride, can we attribute
the opinion the Spaniard holds of his political opponent: "So-
and-so thinks differently from me, so So-and-so is a cuckold
and a bastard." It is vain for one to try to convince him that
the fact that a man supports different principles does not make
him automatically *that*. The only comfort possible is to realize
that So-and-so doubtless holds an equally lively opinion of his
opponent. The adverse judgment is always definitive.

Any permission granted to the collective is based on the
possibility that One may someday be the Other. At bottom,
the rules by which individuals form a civilized society are
motivated by an intelligently understood and organized egoism.
It is logical, most men will agree, that these rules should
prevent my doing whatever I like to So-and-so because, if they
didn't, So-and-so would have the same rights over me. My
limitation implies his limitation, and by restraining myself I am
restraining him.

Such reasoning does not exist for the majority of Spaniards,
who simply cannot conceive of themselves in another man's
position. As reflected in such elegant proverbs as "Who cares
about the other guy," the Spaniard tends to consider every
situation irreversible. For example, only the fear of a fine
prevents the Spanish driver from following his natural impulse
to leave his car blocking another person's car. The other man
can wait until *he* comes back. The possibility of the case being
reversed, that the blocked car might be his own, does not occur
to him. The truck driver who leaves in the middle of the road
the stone he used to wedge his wheel: does he never think that
he might be the driver of the next car?

Or you call a telephone number and—humanly—make a
mistake. Ninety percent of the time, the person at the other end
will say "No" and hang up, leaving you in doubt as to whether
you have made an error in dialing or whether the party has
changed his number. If, in order to avoid another mistake, you

ask "Who is this, please?" the answer will be "What's that to you?" Obviously, it has never occurred to the gentleman or lady who replies so brusquely that the mistake might be his. How is *he* going to make a mistake?

However, this same man or woman will go to a thousand pains to help someone whom he knows, who is "a friend of his." Because it is now a question of a concrete being, of someone with whom he must acquit himself well, not a vague, amorphous part of the Society which gives rights and exacts duties.

The Spaniard answers few letters, and explains this by saying, "I didn't have much to tell you." That is to say, the contents had to be full of "him." The fact that his correspondent waited impatiently for a reply does not seem to worry him unduly. Human relations are, after all, extensions of his own personality. The farther away the other person, the less interest he arouses. Whoever is near, physically, morally, or domestically, enters the charmed circle automatically, and is therefore well-thought-of and kindly treated.[1] If he lives outside he has no value at all, he practically does not exist.

This explains what is an enigma for many foreigners—the incredible difference between the Spaniard's courtesy as seen in his home or at a party, and his behavior in the street. The same person who bows gallantly to kiss the ladies' hands, who rises as soon as someone enters the room, who offers you his house, who shows the greatest interest in attending to people and pleasing them, is a reserved, selfish man outside, who looks on the others who share the world with him as his enemies. He bumps into people without begging their pardon. If someone in the subway complains of being squashed he will tell him to take a taxi; he passes another car on the wrong side at the risk of killing himself; he insults and is insulted. All men are his enemies; even women if they are drivers hear from this "gentleman" malevolent allusions to their mechanical ability. It sometimes happens that after one of these incidents, after the offen-

---

[1] Hence the union among members of a Spanish family. The old folk live with their children and grandchildren; the case seldom arises, as it does in other, richer societies, of their being sent away to an old people's home where "they will be better off."

sive word has been uttered, the protagonists recognize each other; then, as if by magic, comes the smile, the friendly shout— "But man, it's you! Why didn't you say so!" Already in the magic circle again, already united with the other. Now he is a friend. One could not forgive an unknown person for anything, not even for a mistake made in good faith, but one forgives a friend for everything.

The work of the painter, the musician, the scholar, is judged with the same measure of unreason. "That fellow, you think he'll ever do anything good?" It is vain to quote authorities on the subject in support of a good opinion. A person who "makes a bad impression" on a Spaniard is incapable of doing anything important for the rest of his life.

The Englishman says that his home is his castle. He is referring to his individual rights as against the government. The Spaniard also considers his home his castle—but as against everybody—a castle bristling with cannon, surrounded by deep moats. He does not give his name or his address easily. In recent times, I have noticed in the offices of banks, following an American custom, a placard with the employee's name. I feel sure that this innovation has been accepted with disgust and suspicion. In my experience at least, every time when after chatting for some minutes I tried to learn for future use the name of the person I was talking to, I received the same vague reply: "It's not necessary . . . You call and they'll answer you."

And if the Spaniard does not like giving his name, how is he going to give something intimate, his personality? This is the reason for the lack of autobiographies or of love letters in Spanish literature. The man who has worn a cloak for so many years to hide the patches in his trousers is not going to undress spiritually before people he does not know.

The Spaniard's judgments of his fellows are extremely subjective, quite beyond general concepts. A person may be wicked, but if he is *simpático*, if he "goes down well," he is much more accepted in society than one who is virtuous but insipid. If you remind a Spaniard of the immoral qualities of a certain friend, he answers with a smile, "Well, you have to know him. That's how he is," words which irrevocably cancel out any other remark. On the other hand, a Nobel Prize winner may prove *pesado* (boring, dull), an unanswerable phrase with which the Spaniard eliminates another from civil life without allowance of merit or intelligence.

Every Spaniard delights in reading this observation from the work of Valle Inclán: "We Spaniards divide ourselves into two great parties, one the Marquis of Bradomín's and the other all the rest." No reader places himself among "all the rest," naturally. In the same way, the best-remembered dramatic phrase in our literary treasure, "Spain and I are like that, madam," is remembered more for the *I* than for Spain.

When society abets by giving the slightest justification for this pride, the consequences are extreme. The vanity of the Spanish writer who sees his name in the newspaper a couple of times carries him to heights which oblige him to look down on all other writers. Speaking with a number of Spanish writers leads us to the disagreeable conclusion that not one good one exists, for each of them has verbally destroyed every one of his rivals (see Envy).

Quevedo has described a crowd of thirty-two candidates for the same post waiting to hear which of them has obtained it:

> Each one found as many merits in himself as faults in all the others. Each one said to himself that the others were crazy and shameless in seeking what only he deserved. They looked at each other with infernal hatred, their hearts were full of vipers, they prepared infamous affronts to slander one another.
>
> The bores before their eyes increased their spite; they were gnawed by the thought that the post was one and they were many. They became stuck in the arithmetic when they said, "One post between thirty-two, how can there be room for the others?" And they subtracted, "To receive one and pay thirty-two, that cannot be"; and for all of them the "one" was himself and the others the "that cannot be."

When Miguel de Unamuno went to see Alfonso XIII to thank him for a decoration, he said that he deserved it. The king smiled and exclaimed, "The others who are decorated always say they do not deserve it!" "And they are right," answered Unamuno.

"Put yourself in his place" is a meaningless phrase to the Spaniard, for he never identifies himself with another. Why should he do so? He would feel awkward.

A group of ladies go into a cinema. They go in late, because punctuality is not a Spanish defect.[1] The film has already begun, and as they stumble along the center aisle they comment aloud on the scenes appearing on the screen. Note carefully: it is not that they deliberately want to annoy the people who are already seated and attending to what is happening on the screen; it is that they are unaware of the rest of the audience. It is that between the film and them, direct and immediate communication has been established, a communication in no way affected by the society which surrounds them, which is not important, does not exist.

But soon hisses are heard from the public, whose attention has been distracted by these comments spoken out loud. The new arrivals look around, murmur some words of disgust at "people's bad manners" and sit down. Some minutes pass, the ladies become absorbed in the plot, their mouths are shut. Then another group comes down the center aisle. They arrive stumbling, commenting aloud on what appears on the screen. Wrenched out of their stupor, the first group turns around;

[1] This lack of punctuality is another example of pride—it implies scorn for the one who is waiting. The new parish priest of an Andalusian village was surprised to see that funerals were arranged "at seven o'clock for eight." When he asked about this, he was told that the formula was used to ensure attendance. "And if it's going to be at eight in any case, why don't we say at eight?" They stared at him, scandalized. "So that people should come at nine?"

The only punctual spectacle in Spain is the bullfight; an anomaly based on two imperatives: one, to take maximum advantage of the daylight (artificial lighting at the bulls is comparatively recent); the other, more important, to reduce to a minimum what every bullfighter confesses to be the worst time in his life—the moment of waiting, when danger is in the air. When the bull emerges, it is different. The enemy is before him, the bullfighter studies him in the most serene and confident professional manner.

their lips pucker: "Psssst! how frightful, what lack of consideration for others."[1]

Anyone can observe such a scene in Spain, yet it remains
without logical explanation unless we remember that the Spaniard always lives in the present tense, and with his ego always
on his back. Any similarity between the situation in which the
new arrivals find themselves and that of some minutes ago is
pure coincidence. How can *they* be the same as *we*?

The closed world of the Spaniard may be observed in a
thousand details of daily life, even the most superficial ones.
For example, he is walking along a pavement and suddenly—
attracted by a shop window and thereupon remembering something he has to do—he changes direction and crosses diagonally
to the right or left. In any other country in the world, a person
trying to do this would find sprouting in his mind, together with
the wish to change direction, the idea that he might be entering
the path of some other citizen who up to now has been moving
parallel with him. The Spaniard—as in the case of the cinema-
goers—allows no barrier of human society to be interposed
between himself and his object. He crosses imperturbably,
forcing those who find him before them to stop. Sometimes
when this has happened to me, I have pretended not to see the
man crossing and have bumped into him—receiving a look of
extreme annoyance. "But man! What's happening, can't you
see?" The crooked proved to be straight, the irregular normal. . . . He was changing direction, taking the route he ought
to have taken, and no other.

The Spaniard uses adjectives to such an extent that they lose
their true meaning. The word *amigo* (friend), for example, is
so prevalent that when the speaker wants it to refer to a real
friend he has to use *amiguísimo*, or "an intimate friend of

[1] The same principle applies when someone wants to cough. Is he going
to repress it in order not to annoy his neighbors? Andrés Segovia, during
a concert when the coughing was incessant, slowly pulled out a handker-
chief and showed how the noise of a cough could be smothered. There
was great applause, even from those who had been coughing. I imagine
that each of them thought the lesson to be directed at someone else.

mine." There comes a moment when common words no longer represent anything and, thus adulterated, have to be repeated. This is why they speak in Spain of *café-café*, which simply means good coffee as against coffee pronounced only once, which is bad. In the same way they speak of *toro-toro* when the bull has the characteristics of bravery which should logically be found in all bulls used in bullfights.

In other cases it is the facility with which the Spaniard insults that makes it necessary for a word to be repeated if its true meaning is to be conveyed. For instance, "So-and-so is crazy" means no more than that he does things of which the speaker does not approve. Taking into account the fact that the speaker is always sensible, intelligent, and judicious, the other must be raving. Now, if one wants to say that So-and-so is really a psychopathic case, one will have to insist: "So-and-so is crazy, but not crazy—he's crazy-crazy!"

Exaggeration serves the Spaniard's reasoning by multiplying the favorable evidence by a thousand and dividing the damaging testimony in the same proportion. When Brother Bartolomé de Las Casas wanted to demonstrate the Spaniard's cruelty in the Indies he did not mention precise data, which would have been sufficient for his thesis. No. The natives murdered on a particular island came easily to tens of thousands, even though there was only room on the island for tens of hundreds.

The sense of exaggeration increases from north to south, with Andalusians the undisputed masters. "Can't we exaggerate a little?" said a Sevillano when someone pointed out to him the impossibility of putting the five thousand people he had just mentioned into a theater which held one thousand. The good Andalusian refused to let himself be enslaved by arithmetic or geography. He believed in the complete liberty of a man to imagine without pause for practical difficulties.

The tradition is ancient. In the ninth century, Al Juzani told how Al Habid ben Ziyab, a famous judge at Cordova, questioned a witness. "How long have you known about this matter?" The witness answered, "Oh, for a long time, for a hundred years." "How old are you?" "Sixty." "And you've known about this matter for a hundred years? You reckon you knew it forty years before you were born?" "I said this as a comparison," said the witness. "It's a manner of speaking." "In statements by witnesses," replied the judge, "rhetorical figures should not be employed." And he ordered the witness to be flogged, reminding him that another judge, Ibrahim ben Asim ben Asim, had had a man crucified because several witnesses had said that "he was so wicked he deserved to be killed"; it turned out later that they had not really meant that he deserved this punishment or anything like it (see Anger).

In the two cases, the judges were probably not Andalusians. Today in Seville, Cordova, and Malaga, it is possible to testify in this way without such grave consequences, for just as fast as the speaker adds on, the hearer subtracts. If a magistrate hears someone say during a trial that he has known about the matter "for a hundred years," he automatically interprets it as "for quite a long time."

We Spaniards normally believe that what we say is much more interesting than what someone else says, and the proverb insisting that a dialogue is just a monologue with interpolations obviously originated in Spain. When two individuals begin a conversation in a Spanish café, they do not attempt to exchange ideas but to state their own, just so long as the other allows. When one makes the mistake of halting in order to breathe— the good orator breathes without having to pause—his interlocutor takes advantage of the chance to start his own paragraph. In other countries, when two people try to speak at the same time, they say "pardon" and wait; in Spain they also say "pardon" but it is followed by both of them continuing to talk simultaneously. Neither is ever convinced by the reasoning of his opposite; on the contrary, he reaffirms his own convictions with heated improvisation. A discussion enables a man to end up knowing more than he did before, for he has been discovering things out of the invention of his own discussion. De Madariaga has said, "The Spanish thought is born at the moment in which it is manifested. While the Englishman

thinks while acting, the Spaniard thinks while speaking."
Furthermore, the right to discuss is freely accorded to all Spaniards without precedence or hierarchy. This means that an
expert on a subject has no more chance of expressing his
opinion about it without interruption than someone who is
ignorant of it. I have very often heard a man say something like,
"I understand nothing about international politics, but it seems
to me that Communist China . . ." Then, for the space of half
an hour, he tells us his ideas on the subject about which he has
assured us he knows nothing. As Unamuno has said:

> What one does not understand is that a person without
> speaking, or writing, or painting, or sculpturing, or
> playing music, or negotiating affairs, or doing a thing,
> should expect that just because he happens to be there
> he should be taken for a man of extraordinary merit
> and outstanding talent. Nevertheless, here in Spain—
> whether outside it I do not know—not a few examples
> of this most curious occurrence are known.

It is not uncommon in Spain to hear a gentleman answer,
when faced with someone else's doubt, "I'm telling you!"—a
phrase with which he seems to annul all possibility of error. It
is hardly ever a question of a professional opinion (an engineer's on a bridge, a doctor explaining an operation) but of an
opinion on a subject about which both speakers may know
nothing. "I'm *telling* you!"

When a Spaniard is arguing, he admits no points as superior
to his own reasoning. I remember a long controversy about how
a word was spelled. At last the one who was right launched the
missile he had been keeping back for better effect. "Don't argue
any more. That's what it says in the Academy's dictionary."

The other never blinked an eye. "Then the Academy's dictionary is mistaken."

The custom of argument has created a fine verbal proficiency.
The orator is found frequently in cafés and clubs, and when
there was a parliament, facile oratory was considered a most
important quality in a politician. Spaniards demand that the

public speaker (lecturer, radio or television announcer) have
a perfect command of words; the slightest hesitation is enough
to provoke a sarcastic comment on his abilities. (In Anglo-
Saxon countries, on the other hand, phrases are slower and cut
off between "ands" and "ers." As the English are accustomed
to make virtues of their defects, such verbal slowness is considered elegant, and facile eloquence signifies charlatanism.)

> *"He who speaks much errs much*
> *but is right about some things."*

Besides speaking much, the Spaniard speaks very loudly.
There comes a moment when he uses the same tone of voice
for talking as is used in other countries for disputing. Some
years ago a group of Spanish students met in The Hague; intent
on their usual exchange of ideas they did not notice that the
people had disappeared silently and that they were alone in the
big café. A little later police jeeps surrounded the building and
some policemen entered. "What's going on here?" was the first
question.

There was stupefaction, then explanations, apologies by the
police. It turned out that the people in the café had been
listening, at first with curiosity and then with growing alarm,
to the loud tones of the Spanish voices, had seen their violent
gestures, their frowns when underlining difficult points. Historical recollection of the Duke of Alba and his Tercios had
completed the suspicion, and the police had been informed that
"a group of Spaniards are about to pull out their knives in a
downtown café."

By the same token, the Spaniard does not like listening. He
seldom goes to lectures and will not tolerate theatrical functions
if they last too long. (Lope de Vega spoke of "the anger of the
seated Spaniard.") That is why the intermissions between acts
are so important in Spain; each member of the audience can at
last express what he thinks of the author, the play, the
characters, and the actors. It is no accident that the favorite

spectacles in the country are the bulls and football games, events at which the spectator can watch and comment at the same time, take part in the show. For the same reason, the Spaniard prefers drawing-room games which allow him to say and even shout his opinion after each play—dominoes, and such card games as *tute* and *mus*. Silent chess has, naturally, few devotees. As to the diapason with which the Spaniards speak, it is part of the same egotism. Between hearing another finish his argument and imparting one's own valuable opinion to someone who seems prepared to listen to it at the other end of the room, the choice is easy. One raises one's voice a little and that is enough. This experiment, repeated by three or four people, is enough to fill the room with noise. And if someone in the room is being attentive to the radio or the television, he does not beg the talkers to lower their voices; he knows it would be useless. He confines his actions to turning up the loudspeaker.

"In Spain we're all good for everything
even if we're good for nothing."

For workmen, personalization acts in an interesting way. A man who calls a handyman in to repair something has to watch out that he does not make a temporary repair, a botch, because most workmen have no personal pride in anything so impersonal and unimportant. The craftsman, on the other hand, takes pains with his creations because he is behind them, reverberating in their glory.

It shames the Spaniard to have to ask questions in connection with his job, for naturally he must already know everything about it. For several months I had a car which had the defect of spitting out the gasoline pumped into the tank under pressure. Every time I stopped at a gas station I warned the man in charge slowly and precisely: "The trouble is a badly made elbow, take care as it comes out, go very slowly." The attendant usually agreed with a distracted air, while he prepared to put in the hose; my warning appeared unnecessary and more than once

I was reminded of this: "Don't you worry, I've been serving gas for years and years." "But it's different in this case. It leaks a lot." With a confident air he inserted the hose and started pumping. The gas came out violently and spilled on the ground. The mechanic turned toward me. "Here! But it leaks a lot!" "That's what I warned you about." He looked again at the pool on the ground, amazed. "But a lot, a lot. I've never seen such a thing," shaking his head as if before a miracle. I never found an employee who said, "You were right." It was as if on each occasion—and the experience was repeated all over the peninsula—we were speaking different languages. When I said "It leaks a lot" it was not the same as when he said it. When he said it, then *it really was a lot.*

Though this may seem an exaggeration—the personal definition giving reality to things—I have confirmed it in something as simple as the case of names. "That's what Juan told me," says a Spaniard. "What Juan?" says the other, "I don't know any Juan." "Yes, man, the one in the Calle Cea Bermudez, the one who has a bar." "No, I don't know him." "Yes, the one with the scar." "Oh, yes! You mean *Juan!*" Was that not the name? It seems it was not. Until *he* pronounced it, it lacked meaning. This applies, of course, only if he remembers the name—very often he cannot think of it.

One is not surprised, then, at the number of gatherings where someone will say something bad about a family or a profession without knowing that one of its representatives is before him. "You know what introductions are," he explains later. "One doesn't notice names." Obviously. How is *one* going to notice the names of *others?*

> *"Doctors and lawyers,*
> *may God deliver us from the best."*

Spaniards apply such terms as "quack" or "charlatan" even to the best-known professionals. They regard those who dedicate themselves to branches of culture other than their own with a mixture of commiseration and irony, like the condescension with which one regards those who apply themselves to something not very serious and, of course, within anybody's reach. A famous writer, Wenceslao Fernández Flórez, told me of the many times a friend had spoken to him of his own literary possibilities. "No," the man had said, "the fact is I haven't time. But I know a story, something which happened to a maid of mine, which I tell you would make a great novel. . . . But I haven't the time."

Never for one moment had it occurred to him that he would not know how to write it. And with the same marvelous condescension, he had said, "Send me your book, man. I promise to read it." A promise which he imagined would send the author mad with joy. In the case of a painter, he would have asked for a canvas: "Send me a picture. I promise to frame it."

If a Spaniard's judgments are pronounced with regard to books he has not read or a painting he does not understand, they become even more heated in the case of films. For the Spaniard may be ignorant of the bookshop or the picture gallery, but he is an assiduous film-goer. Spain is the second country in Europe in proportion of money spent on the cinema. The Spaniard likes the movies, and he likes displaying his culture and erudition to the family accompanying him. The Eiffel Tower never appears on the screen without six or seven gentlemen saying gravely to their wives, "Paris." The wife nods, delighted to know that her husband is so well informed.

I remember when Antonioni's *The Eclipse* was shown in Spain. It is an unusual film and presupposes a certain sophistication in the spectator if he is to understand and like it. In other countries it produced a mixed reaction; some were enthusiastic and others went out determined never to see anything like it again.

But in Spain this second and more numerous section of the public reacted as if it had been insulted. Their thinking went more or less as follows: "I am an intelligent and cultured man and I understand films. I do not understand this film. It is therefore obvious that the fault is in the film, that it is nothing but a leg-pull, a hoax." I personally heard a gentleman distinguished for his amiability and sense of humor say sarcastically to a young man who applauded at the end of the show, "You must be very intelligent."

Nowhere is literary judgment so easy as in Spain. Once there was a radio broadcast in which a group of writers commented on Pasternak's *Doctor Zhivago*. The criticisms were stern, so cutting and negative that a lady in the group, who had a foreign accent that was probably Russian, was surprised and asked humbly, "But how can you judge it like that? In what part of the book have you read that?"

"I haven't read the book, señora," was the amazing reply. It turned out that of the four writers who had met to discuss it, only she had read it.

A similar phenomenon was described more than a century ago when Mesonero y Romanos wrote of a bookshop: "There is a group of literary men who constantly occupy the rickety benches near the counter; when someone enters to ask for a book, the said literary men criticize it and make comments on it, and say that it is not anything much, and after having judged it at their pleasure ask the bookseller to lend them a copy to read."

The number of people who have returned from places without ever having been to them is infinite. Any attempt to explain something to a person vaguely familiar with it is considered intolerable vanity. A friend of mine once said goodbye when I was going to Italy as a correspondent.

"You're not going to describe the Sistine Chapel to us, are you?"

"No," I said, "you tell me what it's like."

He did not know.

To accuse a Spaniard of being mistaken when he is describing something serves to infuriate rather than to correct him. I remember a writer years ago who was telling me the plot of his historical novel. King James I and his court at Saragossa were mentioned continually in the narrative. "And then he returned to his capital. . . . to Saragossa. . . ." The third time I interrupted him.

"Excuse me. James I didn't have his capital at Saragossa."

"Very well . . . But he went there often." And he went on with his narrative. Later he said I was a pedant.

"Better to be a cuckold without anyone knowing than not to be one when everyone thinks you are."

The fear of ridicule is firmly rooted in the Spanish personality and governs most of his reactions. The serious thing is not that something is bad but that one's neighbor considers it so, and even the bad is not so serious as the ludicrous. The mere possibility of being mocked by others impels the Spaniard to violence (see Anger). "So I shall put you to death here, that you may not know that I know that you know my weaknesses," says Segismundo to the terrified Rosaura, who has overheard a soliloquy in which he bewailed his luck; it is an obligation, a sacrosanct duty when honor is involved. The fear of ridicule impels the characters of the Calderonian dramas to murder their guilty wives, and the appearance of that guilt is enough to unleash the revenge. When a Spaniard finds out that his wife is deceiving him he is distressed not so much because of the trust betrayed as because he feels helpless, naked before the world surrounding him. His dignity, the luxurious dress with which he covers his defects and stains, has been wrested from him.

With the passing of time the bloody revenge has ceased in most cases, but the jealous vigilance remains. Spanish jealousy has its foundations in pride, not in love. Do not look at another man (or another woman). Why? Because I love you so much that it gives me pain to see you set your eyes on someone else? No, because you make me ridiculous. The sight of a former boyfriend of the woman he has married generally upsets the Spaniard, not because he believes that there are still live coals where there was once fire, or if he does that these coals may flare up again with the new contact. Rather, he imagines that the other man will relive amorous moments with his beloved and will thereby push *him* into the background. The other knew her first. . . . And the more affectionate "the other" is to him, the worse. What is this? Protection? Pity? Two words which irritate the average Spaniard to distraction.

The avoidance of ridicule becomes a very broad concept. The Spaniard pays the restaurant bill almost without reading it, for to study it would be a sign of meanness. Why? Because the spendthrift tradition is considered good form. In *La Fonda Nueva*, Larra gives us a pathetic description:

> That young man who came in meant to eat for half a duro but he found twenty acquaintances at a neighboring table; he let himself be caught by his black sense of honor, because his acquaintances had ordered food worth a duro. If instead it had been a woman he wanted to conquer who was eating at the other table, he would have ordered a doubloon's worth.

The squire of *Lazarillo de Tormes* who walks past people with a toothpick in his mouth to pretend he has eaten can be taken as a commonly repeated and symptomatic example. And to avoid ridicule, the characters in Taboada's stories shut themselves up in their house to pretend to be having a summer holiday they cannot afford, or the women are killing themselves with sewing at home to avoid the humiliation of "my daughters working" publicly and openly. Today it is normal for them to do so; still, however, "My wife work? What will people say?"

"A well-dressed man is received everywhere."

The use of the cloak, kept up for so many years despite changing fashions, represented a compromise between pride and poverty, which are often brothers in Spain. For the cloak was the ideal solution for appearing elegant without any need to spend money on clothes; who knew what there was underneath, what darnings, ragged elbows, frayed shirts? The cloak provided elegance, dignity, but above all, security.

"All these grave personages," said Theophile Gautier of the

Puerta del Sol in Madrid, "stand wrapped up in their cloaks, although it is frightfully hot, on the frivolous pretext that what keeps out the cold keeps out heat as well." Above all it kept out the curious and critical gaze of other people.

The disappearance of the cloak at the beginning of this century complicated matters, but the Spaniard withstood it heroically. Appearances are sacred in Spain, and anyone who judges village life by the human aspect of the principal streets would believe that Spain has one of the highest standards of living in the world. In comparison with their incomes, Spaniards spend much more on dress than do the citizens of other countries, and anyone who establishes a direct relationship between their appearance and their daily life makes a mistake. Spanish homes are hardly ever on the level of their owners' appearance. Many foreigners are surprised at how reluctant the Spaniard is to invite a stranger to his home, yet willing to take him to the best shows and the most expensive restaurants. The reason is often that the rooms in his house are gloomy, the furniture ugly, comfort nonexistent. "As we never invite anyone, why should we wish for more?" For many years there was a special room only for visits, hermetically sealed from the family. It was the most beautiful room and was used only to impress outsiders.

Pérez Galdós describes a family in the greatest misery. They are continually having to pawn things, from jewelry to cloaks, but there is something which Doña Pura, the lady of the house, flatly refuses to touch even if she starves to death:

> The best room! Pawn something from the best room! The idea always caused Doña Pura terror and shudders, for the best room was the part of the ménage nearest to her heart, the true symbolic evidence of the domestic hearth. It contained pretty furniture . . . chairs upholstered in damask . . . silk curtains—Doña Pura esteemed those curtains as highly as the fabric of her heart. And when the specter of necessity appeared to her and whispered in her ear the terrible figures of the next day's economic battle, Doña Pura shivered with

fright and said, "No, no, the shirts rather than the curtains." To strip the bodies seemed a tolerable sacrifice to her, but to strip the best room—never that!

The fear of ridicule restrains the Spaniard's fancies about dress. The primary consideration is "gravity and the fear of God," said a sixteenth-century phrase. Now, as then, Spaniards lag behind fashion and are often disgusted when there are changes in the style and color of clothes, only falling in with these changes when they have lost impact and aggressiveness. The Spaniard's ideal of dress is to be prominent among those who at first sight pass unnoticed (this does not apply to the women, who, like women in all parts of the world, are eager to attract looks), but to "call attention" is still regarded as bad form.

This sober tradition goes far back. In the ninth century, Al Juxani described someone's proposing to the Cordovan Yahya ben Yahya that he introduce in Spain the turban worn in the East, assuring him that the Spanish people would follow him.

"I don't believe it," answered Yahya. "Ben Baxir wore silk clothes and the people have not imitated him, and Ben Baxir was a man with sufficient prestige to impose the fashion. If I wore a turban, people would leave me to wear it alone and would not imitate me."

Nine centuries later, a minister who was more certain than Yahya of what the example of a highly placed man was worth, tried to change the dress style of the people of Madrid. The fashion then was to be decked out in a great cloak and a broad-brimmed hat, two garments that covered a sizable part of the body and made the identification of criminals difficult. The Marquis of Esquilache decided that all the inhabitants of Madrid should change to the French style of short cloak and three-cornered hat. It was put in an edict. No one followed it. The minister insisted by putting patrols of troops in the streets, each accompanied by a tailor; every Madrileño dressed in the old fashion was pushed into a doorway by the soldiers. The tailor cut short the cloak and pinned up the brim of his hat, thus converting it into a tricorne. The people were so annoyed that they rushed into the streets in a movement of armed protest, later known as the Esquilache riots, and the minister had to leave his post. Although political causes were concealed in the movement, the masses reacted from a pure spirit of indignation at a general order against the individuality of their clothing. It is perhaps the only riot in the world that originated as the result of a fashion.

(Actually, the minister's style of dress was imposed soon afterward by another minister acting more politically than his predecessor. As he could not make the new dress "sympathetic," he managed to make the old one antipathetic. The executioner of Madrid, a personage who was always hated by the mob, walked ostentatiously through the streets of the capital with a hat and a long flowing cloak. This exhibition was enough to make many Madrileños begin to loathe the traditional style.)

The fear of appearing in an unfavorable or not very attractive light produces one of the positive effects of Spanish pride, for it has done much to reduce in Spain a social sickness extensive throughout the world. I refer to drunkenness. A people who begin to drink wine at the age of eight surprise foreigners, especially Anglo-Saxons, by the small number of drunks in the streets or at parties. "He doesn't know how to drink" is enough to shut the door of a house to a man. (Those who know no more of Spain than the festival of Pamplona will find it difficult to believe this statement, but we must remember the escapist character of those particular days and the higher consumption of alcohol in the north, where the strict Catholic vigilance against another sin, that of lust, forces the robust Basque to seek the release of song and wine for his tremendous vigor and strength.)

The repeated use of the expression *qué dirán*, "what they will say," has led to its becoming a noun. *El qué-dirán* influences, dictates, advises the actions of most Spanish men. When a Spanish girl loses her virtue, her first reaction is "What will you think of me?"

"There are some very honest people who although they are

starving would prefer outsiders not to feel sorry for them,"
wrote St. Teresa, and her reference is not confined to her time,
which is that of the best-known example of concealed poverty,
the hidalgo of *Lazarillo*.

The terror of the poor Spaniard of good family at having to
reveal his needs has lasted to our own day, and the name by
which such people are designated has a definite place in the
vocabulary of charity. They are the *vergonzantes*, "ashamed
ones," those who are ashamed to ask for alms, who stay on in
an old house at the old rent, hoping that someone will remember them without their having to look that person in the face.
Their type would be strange elsewhere, but it is logical in Spain.

The most popular jokes circulating in a country should be
taken more seriously than they are. Most stories which become
popular presuppose acceptance of the point on the part of the
masses, and are explained by the public's identification with
the portrait of a type contained within that public. This seems
to me quite clear with regard to a little story which illustrates
the importance for Spaniards of *qué dirán*. The story tells of a
group of parachutists of various nationalities who jump from
the plane only when the sergeant touches the button that makes
their particular sensibility react. The Spaniard refuses to jump,
and all appeals to his patriotism and to loyalty to the head of
the state are useless. At last the sergeant exclaims, "The fact is
you're a coward!" "I, a coward? Look—without a parachute!"
And he jumps. Every time I have heard this story told I have
seen pleased, assenting smiles around me. Yes sir, that's what
we're like.

I am firmly convinced that the value of the Spanish soldier in
battle owes much more to this negative concept than to any
positive one such as love of country or fidelity to any oath he
has taken. Any ex-combatant of the Civil War will tell you that
the most effective threat with which to spur men into combat
was always the possible criticism of others. What will they think
of us? Are you going to be outdone by C company? Are you
going to let them leave us behind? (The Italian, on the other
hand, is quite different. He has no feeling of emulation, and

the fact that C company should overtake him seems irrelevant to him. However, his sporting spirit makes him an extraordinary individual hero. During the last war, daring Italian airmen and submariners offered a curious contrast to the Italian armies surrendering en masse.)

"Let me die, let my fame live," said the ancient Spaniards, and the men of today seem to be echoing them.

One of the Spaniards most representative of the seventeenth century was Captain Alonso de Contreras, who left some memoirs which are as incredible as they are truthful. In them he tells what it was that induced him on one occasion to help a compatriot in a fight, not knowing who was in the right or how the thing had started. "So as not to lose face, we said, 'Come on, to hell with it!' " He nearly lost his life in the fight.

> *"Win good fame and lie down to sleep;*
> *win bad fame and lie down to die"*

In the seventeenth century Quevedo bewailed this enslavement to honor:

> What shall I say, then, of honor? That it causes the most tyrannies in the world and the most harm, and hinders the most delights. A poor gentleman is starving, he has nothing to wear, his clothes are tattered and patched, perhaps he becomes a thief; yet he does not ask for anything because he says he has honor, nor does he want to serve, because he says it is dishonorable. Men say that everything they seek and toil for is to maintain honor. For honor's sake a man does not eat what he wants to when he knows very well where he could. For honor's sake the widow dies between her lifelong walls. For honor's sake, without knowing what a man or a pleasure is, the young lady spends thirty years married to herself. For honor's sake the married woman eliminates whatever desires she is asked not to have. For honor's sake men cross the sea. For honor's sake one man kills another. For honor's sake they all

spend more than they have. And honor, in all this, is a stupidity for body and soul, for it takes from the one its pleasures and from the other its rest. And so that you may see how unhappy you men are and the great danger that threatens what you most prize, you must be warned that the things you most value are honor, life and property; and honor is bound up with women's backsides, life is in the hands of the doctors, and property in the pen of the scriveners.

In the eighteenth century Cadalso wrote:

One of the reasons for the decadence of the arts in Spain is doubtless the repugnance which every son feels at following his father's career. In London, for example, we find a shoemaker's shop which has been passed down from father to son for five or six generations. But in this country every father wants to place his son higher up, and if he does not the son takes good care to leave his father lower down; and with this method no family fixes itself in any particular branch of business.

This still is true today. I remember the enthusiasm with which the chauffeur of a family who are friends of mine spoke to me of his son's future. "He won't be a mechanic like me, sir, he's started to work in an office." I asked him what wages he was earning, as I imagined they would be far below those of a mechanic. But that did not matter to the father. The boy wore a tie and an ordinary suit at his work. He was already of another social class.

"The heavens do not give love without jealousy."

Because the Spaniard finds it so hard to put himself in someone else's position, another person's amorous sentiments are easily considered pretentious. On principle, every feeling that one does not share is pretentious, as are the ways in which it is expressed.

Madariaga maintains that the Spaniard's jealousy is a product of envy. I insist it is the fruit of pride. Envy presupposes desire, and the Spaniard continues being jealous long after he has ceased to be physically interested in a girl. It annoys him to be supplanted in his own field, in the garden which was his and in which he walked as lord. If the average Spaniard could, he would do with his ex-girlfriends what Philip IV did with his: send them to a convent once his interest in them was over.

This pride also acts in the supplanter, who is greatly irritated that there should have been someone before himself enjoying the same conditions of confidence with his beloved. As I have said, many arguments are born of a mere meeting with the wife's former loved one. The Spaniard who first knew her, while he does not dare say so, in his heart would be delighted if she could again emerge each afternoon from her finishing school as in the old days to meet *him* and learn from him and only from him what is important in life.

As has often been observed, the Spaniard does not say to a woman *te amo* (I love you), but *te quiero* (I want you), which is a possessive verb implying authority over property not to be shared with anybody and presupposing many more rights than duties. In love as in other manifestations, the Spaniard personifies what is objective; the surroundings, the buildings, the whole world only exist to authenticate his feelings.

Perhaps this feeling explains better than moral considerations, which do not restrict Spaniards in their intimate life, why such a poor view is taken of displaying love in public. A pair of lovers holding hands is enough to provoke a smile, not of pleasant understanding but of sarcasm. Do they have to make an exhibition of themselves? And naturally a closer contact earns an anathema. Although years have passed since Fernández Flórez in his *Relato Inmoral* showed the difficulties two lovers run into when trying to be alone and affectionate—what with the indignant reaction of passersby, coachmen, or authorities of all kinds—the behavior of Spanish couples in public is even today probably the most meritorious of any in the civilized world. I repeat that this is due to the Spaniard's inability to imagine himself someone else.

The best way to understand others is to remember one's own experience. "We've all been children," observe grown-ups before a piece of childish mischief. "We've all been young" before a pair of lovers? Never!

> If I see you speaking to another
> I swear to you by Jesus
> that at the door of your house
> there'll have to be a cross.

This Andalusian *soleá* (a kind of song) is an exaggeration only as regards the punishment, not the feeling that inspires it. No one invents such a wish who does not have it immediately inside him.

> I am jealous of the air
> that touches your face
> if the air were a man
> I would kill him!

> *or*

> If I knew the stones
> my love walks on in the street
> I'd turn them upside down
> so that no one should tread them.

Such sentiments do not inspire the Spaniard to hurl himself at the throat of anyone who chats with his girl. Time and circumstances have changed that. But if he could make an intruder disappear into thin air by looking at him, he would think it a very good thing.

It happens that modern customs move in a direction contrary to the Spaniard's feelings. As there is a *qué dirán* with regard to what is out of date, many lovers, like many fathers, reluctantly accept a family situation to which they are opposed on principle. In other words, García Lorca's Bernarda Alba does not exist in Spain today. Not even in small villages is there a mother who curbs the lively temperaments of her daughters to such an extent. But at heart I am sure that many mothers and fathers understand Bernarda, sympathize with her, and only the fear of ridicule—old fogy, out-of-date!—prevents their imitating her in the treatment of their daughters, whose growing they watch with both love and fear.

"When the fig tree is budding, lock up the maidens."

> *"The smoke of my native land*
> *shines more than the fire of others."*

With respect to Spain vis-a-vis other countries, all Spaniards react similarly, however different their education and their way of life: the refined international traveler responds in the same way as the yokel who has never left his village. Let us look, for example, at Juan Valera, a diplomat, a man given to the classics, whom no one can censure for chauvinism when he writes about an American book, *The Land of the Castanet* by H. G. Chatfield Taylor: "Another terrible mania of Mr. Taylor's is the one he displays against bullfights, to which he went nevertheless and which he enjoyed watching. The fact is that I like these fights so little that I never go to them any more than, when in the U.S.A., I go to amuse myself by watching two citizens break each other's sternums and jawbones with punches for the delight of the cultivated spectators; but I will not therefore say that while such a sport is fashionable among the Yankees, they can never become civilized but will go on being barbarous and ferocious. Mr. Taylor, on the other hand, declares that we, only because we tolerate bullfights, are incapable of civilization in its highest sense."

The note is revealing. Sr. Valera, as a Spaniard, can stay away from bullfights and even loathe them, but that a foreigner, an outsider, should describe and criticize them exasperates him. Ortega y Gasset, the most European of our twentieth-century intellectuals, wrote to the same effect in his "Preface to an Englishwoman Who Does Not Like Bullfights."

When Spanish pride shows its house to a foreigner, it always does so in the certainty that it is showing something new to the visitor, who should in no way attempt to change from spectator to participant. When somebody, nearly always Anglo-Saxon,

tries to show his enthusiasm by taking an active part, the reaction is usually cold. An American girl applauding Flamenco
dancing is regarded with pleasure. The same girl hurling herself
onto the boards and trying to imitate the steps produces
consternation and sarcasm. It seems to the Spaniard that something very much his own is being caricatured, and he does not
like this at all.

I remember an American who was going to ride in the Casa
de Campo park in Madrid. He had a boy of about ten and had
dressed him *de corto*, the Andalusian horseman's style. The
boy was fair, chubby, with blue eyes, and he rode his horse
very seriously in his broad hat, short jacket and *zajones* (leather
chaps over the trousers), following his father who was rigged
out in the same way. I am sure the good gentleman was convinced that his desire to "go native" would earn him the
sympathy of everyone. What he actually earned was muffled
irritation. "Have you seen," the stable boy said to me, "have
you seen the little booby? I could kick him in the backside!"

The same thing occurs at the bulls, where everyone with a
foreign accent is automatically excluded from knowledge of
what happens in the ring, however much he may have studied
and watched the brave fiesta. It is as if the whole treasury of
Spanish folklore were prohibited to those who have not had
the luck to be born here; if they had, that fact would automatically confer technical knowledge about wine, dancing, bulls
and Flamenco singing.

When the Spaniard goes abroad he always finds himself
slightly uncomfortable. Apart from the fact that he speaks in a
voice louder than is normal in other countries, there is something of embarrassment in his whole attitude. It is the embarrassment of one who knows he is in somebody else's yard (and
let's not forget that for a Spaniard what is somebody else's is
altogether different).[1] At heart, when he compares his civilization and culture with those of other European countries, he

---

[1] Some refuse to emerge from their protective shell. It is said of the
bullfighter Guerra that, before a bullfight in the South of France, he
was greeted by a compatriot, "How's things, maestro?" "Well, as you
see," answered Guerra, "here I am surrounded by foreigners!"

feels an uneasiness which, typically, he does not hide but rather displays, indulging not in discretion but in bravado. I remember a group on a street in Copenhagen. They were walking along with their hands in their pockets (restless hands are one of the Spaniard's characteristics); they stopped often, to the consternation of the other passersby, who did not understand that a street is not a route of travel but a promenade for taking a stroll; they thumped each other on the back; they made mocking comments on what they saw. It seemed that by shouting they were manifesting a personality which they felt weakened without the support of familiar things. At times they sought an explanation for their feelings of inferiority. "The fact is," one of them told me, "foreigners envy us because we've got more guts! Because we discovered America!"

As the Spaniards are a people of contrasts, there also exists, in a minority, the type who remains stupefied before a bulldozer and shakes his head with a pessimistic air, saying, "When shall we have something like that in Spain? We're a miserable lot. . . ." Yet even in this last case, the foreigner should refrain from agreeing with him if he does not want to end their friendship.

In principle the Spaniard—as a good, proud man—is stubborn about displaying his admiration. A car of the latest model will attract the looks of a few technicians, but the man in the street is annoyed if he is caught staring at something "like a yokel." There are few places in the world where movie stars can move as freely as in Spain. Only in the case of those who really are idols of the masses (Cantinflas, Jorge Negrete) is there a tightly pressed crowd trying to get near the figures. (Do not confuse the spectacle of a star's arrival at an airport with a true public riot. These "spontaneous" demonstrations are organized with the greatest care, from the shout which those present must utter to the price of the broken plate glass, which the movie producer will gladly pay the airport.) The Spaniard hardly ever asks for autographs, unlike his contemporaries in other countries, for it seems undignified to him. And in reading interviews with actors of international renown in Spanish journals,

I always seem to note a hostility toward the person being inter-
viewed, as if the journalist wanted to make him pay for the
humiliation of having to devote so much time to him. More
typical, however, is the deprecatory comment with which the
Spaniard tries to forgive himself for having yielded to the
impulse of curiosity: it is easy to hear said of a famous actress,
"She's not so pretty as all that," or of an actor, "How he's
aged." And this extends to the lowest grade of society. López
Rubio told me that when he brought into Spain a red torpedo-
shaped sports car, something never seen hitherto in the country,
he heard a ragged lad say, "I've got three like that at home!"

And when for obvious reasons the Spaniard cannot know
more than the person he is talking to, will he admit the gap in
his knowledge? No; Antonio Machado, who knew us very well
(see Envy), described what happens in two famous lines:

> Wretched Castile, that ruled but yesterday,
> wrapped in its rags, despises what she doesn't know.

And as there are many things the Spaniard does not know,
his contempt must nearly always be general for what is outside
his immediate range of experience. An adventurer may travel
to the most obscure and inhospitable regions of the Amazon and
undergo incredible experiences. If on his return he announces a
lecture on this subject, the hall will be half empty. Nobody is
interested in listening to someone talk on a subject he does not
know well enough to offer criticism, to answer at the end, to
interrupt. And if one is not to interrupt, what is the point of
listening?

Américo Castro points to the great scarcity of travel literature by Spaniards; there is little ambition to compose a geography, a geology or a history of a foreign country. Their cultural
pride finds it natural that there should be Hispanic experts in
Sweden, in Japan, in Russia, but does not find it odd that in
Spain there hardly exist specialists even in French or English
literature.

And to the villager it seems natural and usual that the
foreigner should jabber Spanish (which is characterized—this

could not be more symbolic—as "speaking like a Christian"). I have often noticed, when accompanying tourists in Spain, that peasants are surprised at their ignorance.

"But he must speak *some* Spanish . . ."

"No, not a word. Don't you realize they speak English in his country?"

"How strange . . ."

And they shake their heads as they look at him. The farm laborer of today knows that his cousin sailed away to the Americas, "where they speak the same as us." He does not need any other details to imagine that this is how it is all over the world.

On the other hand, Spanish pride makes every foreigner a guest. I know of no other people with a broader conception of hospitality, more so in the street, the bar and the restaurant than at home, for reasons already mentioned. So deeply rooted is this obligation of the host that in restaurants, in that graceful struggle to obtain the bill, it is typical everywhere for the native to tell the waiter in an undertone, "The gentleman is a foreigner," and for the bill to come directly into his hands.

And curiously enough, the hospitality increases among the lower social classes. Third-class male passengers offer with obvious good will the food which their wives have prepared for them, and I have advised my German, Italian, and American students at least to taste it if they do not want to offend. (To what will this offense be due? To the contempt implied[1] or to the mistrust which this contempt suggests?) Américo Castro has pointed out the Arab influence in the custom of offering what one is eating. It is also obvious that hospitality is greater in poor lands, where people come to your house to find food and water. It is also possible that the indignant reaction of the man who sees his offering refused goes back to stories of poisons offered with a smile on tables covered with splendid viands.

Walter Starkie, the author of *Don Gitano*, has told us that

[1] Eating with someone indicates familiarity and trust, important elements in a hierarchic society. That is why, when someone displays a friendship for which there has been no cause, he is asked sarcastically, "Where have we eaten together?"

many times when he was going to pay for a glass of wine in a miserable roadside inn he found it already paid for by a humble muleteer who was playing cards in a corner. The innkeeper nearly always explained, "He didn't know you, but he saw you were a foreigner."

The Spaniard likes to play the host because every Spaniard bears within him a Duke of Osuna *manqué*. (The duke was an ambassador to Russia delightfully remembered for having thrown his gold dinner service into the Moscowa after it had been used once at a party, a gesture which in other countries would be considered madness.) But in this matter of the treatment of the foreigner, one will do well always to remember that he is foreign. When the new arrival, deceived by the cordiality and confidence with which the native speaks to him, starts expounding his opinions on the life and politics of the country, he will immediately notice a cooling of the atmosphere. The most anti-Franquista of Spaniards refuses to accept a foreigner's criticism of the head of the state. Government propaganda had only to blow lightly on already red-hot coals to produce a reaction against the United Nations' decisions with regard to Spain. "These guys are going to come and tell us what to do!" people said. Note that they did not even discuss whether the decisions were right or wrong. They refused to accept the possibility that anyone from so far away could tell them how to govern themselves.

When political beliefs and age-old resentments are combined with local pride, a person can feel threatened even when no one has dreamed of threatening him. This is frequently the case in Catalonia, where local pride resents anything that Castilian pride may accomplish.

I remember a Catalan farmer who lived in Arenys de Munt. He was a cultured man, well informed about the world's problems, but when referring to Spain he always spoke with a grudge. "Don't deceive yourself," he said to me one day, "there's a plan in Madrid to crush Catalonia in five years' time." "Look," I replied, "if there were in Madrid a plan for anything organized with such precision and certainty, it wouldn't be Madrid."

For in Madrid, as in a great part of Spain, pride and hauteur are touched with frivolity. All hatred of control, of domination, refers to the moment when the possibility is expressed, and usually ends there. When a Spaniard says, "Nobody can do that to me! I won't tolerate it from you," he is obeying an instinct as short on aspirations as it is violent. I mean to say that once the explosion has passed, the Spaniard will not seek the means to prevent that oppression, that outrage. For this would imply organization, collectivity, and collectivity always signifies a process in which each component has to abandon part of its own personality, the better to fit in with the whole. And this is a lot to ask of a Spaniard.

I believe this explains the seemingly incongruous fact that Spanish individual pride has accepted a dictatorship for so many years (over three regimes—of the Right, the Left, and the Right again—there are Spaniards who have had forty years of it). Throughout the present regime, the government has understood two important characteristics of the Spaniard. First, that it is impossible to shut his mouth. For many years in the cafés, among theater audiences, at parties, people have talked in a way which would have been impossible under the regimes of Hitler, Mussolini, Stalin or Perón.

And the regime has allowed it because it knows—the second characteristic—that this self-indulgence is purely verbal and that the Spaniard, having expressed his ideas on the subject in cutting and nearly always obscene words, thereby terminates his civic protest. He retains a quiet conscience. That his words are not to be enacted in any change is a secondary problem, somebody else's. He has said what he thinks.

After all, so long as it does not touch him precisely, what happens to others leaves him carefree. And the rest think likewise, each one is a monad, a unity outside the collectivity, and as such has no conscience of its own. Not even in the Civil War were there two truly allied blocks. Ten groups on one side fought against ten groups on the other, each thinking he was fighting for his own unique cause and that his allies of the moment "would see what was right all in good time."

And the censorship? The censorship is always thought to

affect an individual, never the people as a whole. The masses
are denied something to be seen or read, but as they do not
know what it is, they cannot react. Nor is there admiration for
the writer, who in France, for instance, makes the whole country feel the injury caused the intellectual (a type who is regarded
in Spain with certain misgivings, "one of those writing fellows,
a loafer, really!" as the concierge said in one of Tono's
comedies).

The greater patriotism is naturally succeeded by a lesser,[1]
reducing the geographical area but maintaining the same
ferocious feeling of churlish independence. The most famous
exploits in Spanish history involve the defense not of a land but
of a city: Saragossa, Gerona, Sagunto, Numancia. In other
wars—the Napoleonic generals said admiringly—it was sufficient to win one battle for the whole country to realize how
useless it was to go on fighting. But in Spain, the lack of unity
produced island after island of resistance, for what the native
was defending was part of himself, and so long as he had
anything left he would defend it to the death. Which he did on
many occasions.

The foreigner should not speak evil of Spain even if the
Spaniard has just been cursing it; neither can the dweller in
Upper San Juan allow himself jests about Lower San Juan in
front of one of its natives. The quarrels between neighboring
enemies occur throughout Spanish history and in literature,
from the episode of the ass's braying in *Quixote* to the fight
between the men of Lorío and those of Entralgo in the *Aldea
perdida* of Palacio Valdés.

When authority is divided between towns (the capital of the

---

[1] In some cases it replaces it, as when the Spaniard goes abroad and,
instead of meeting with his compatriots in a *Casa de España*, does so in
one *de Galicia* or *de Asturias*. It is the intermediate solution, the compromise between the centrifugal longing of individualism and the wish
to fraternize with his fellow countrymen. Madariaga maintains that the
two most constant characteristics of the Spaniard are separatism and
dictatorship, both of which are found, with even greater virulence than
on the peninsula, in the Latin American countries.

province and the most important industrial city, or the episcopal seat and the political headquarters), hatreds are produced which make the feuds of Capulet and Montague seem laughable. Paco Vighi told me that on the occasion of the festival of Palencia, a time when the most arrogant city is pleased to welcome the stranger, there appeared in the packed bull ring a placard which said, "Palencia greets all visitors except those from Valladolid."

Local pride needs no special foundation. If a town or a village is ugly, its mineral wealth is praised; or an old castle or ruins of a monastery (one of those which people boast about without having done a thing to forestall its ruin); or, naturally, the exploits of the local football team. If there is nothing at all in the present, there always remain the history and the illustrious sons of the town. Spain has been so prodigal of saints and heroes that there is ever some figure ready at hand in moments of difficulty, should someone offend the inhabitants.

When Victor de la Serna wrote his famous *Journey through Spain*, he described each one of the small villages he found in such beautiful terms as to make the reader believe he was dealing with another Spain. In his pages nearly everything turned out to be beautiful, manly, sweet or severe, always thrilling. The inhabitants of *these* villages did not write to thank him for his words, because they found them natural and logical. But if at the end of an eulogistic paragraph he said, for example, "What a pity that this beauty is sullied by the state of the streets," he received indignant missives: How dare he speak like that of the place where Brother Benito de los Cantos was born? Who did he think he was?

The Spanish capitals are oversensitive because, among other things, the censorship over the last twenty-five years has not allowed people to befoul with irony what must be the perfect state of the nation to all natives and foreigners. They are up in arms at the slightest allusion that might be considered offensive, and there are no gibes even in humorous media. The weekly *La Codorniz* once published an article which referred in passing to a young lady who made no distinction between "a fair man

from London and a dark man from Murcia." The editor of the
paper, Alvaro de Laiglesia, received dozens of indignant letters
from the city in question, culminating in a telegram saying, "If
you are a man, come to Murcia."

In his *Memorias*, Baroja has described a telling incident:
"Three or four of us, friends, went to Granada. . . . It was cold.
One morning we were in the Alhambra. I said, 'If there were
no curtains or windows or something of the kind in these rooms
in the time of the Moors, the Mahomets and Boabdils would
have died of cold.' This no doubt offended local patriotism, and
some days later they sent me a letter with pretensions to irony
and some little woolen underpants."

When some years ago a priest wrote a book casting doubt on
whether St. Teresa had been born in Avila, the wrath of that
city was extraordinary. None who spoke or wrote about the
work mentioned the documents it presented. St. Teresa came
from Avila and that was enough.

Local pride surpasses itself when political circumstances make
a place a center to which other inhabitants of the country have
to come if they want to solve their problems. This is the case
of the city-state known as Madrid. (The pride of Barcelona or
Bilbao is more regional and almost racial. People boast more
of being Catalans or Basques than of being citizens of one city
or another. And Seville is different again. While people in
Barcelona and Bilbao spend the day comparing their characteristics with those of Madrid, Seville lives completely outside
the dispute. For Seville, Madrid is the same as Bilbao or
Barcelona: they are all cities without enchantment or grace, all
of them cities with the grave defect of not having a district
called Triana or of not being on the Guadalquivir.)

The pride of Madrid began in earnest when Philip II declared
the city his capital, and it has not stopped growing since then.
There is the proverbial phrase "from Madrid to heaven," and
another one, "and in heaven a little hole to see Madrid." There
is the incredible sermon, related by the Frenchman Burgoyne
in the eighteenth century, in which the priest announced that
when Jesus was being tempted he was lucky that the Pyrenees

hid Madrid from him, for if not he would probably have accepted the gift and humiliated himself before the devil.

Madrid has grown as the Spanish population and its problems have increased, and there are very few on its soil who are Madrileños of two or three generations. But that doesn't matter. The son of the Asturian feels himself completely Madrileño, as does the man who was born in Galicia and arrived in the capital as a child. The feeling that this is a most important club, to which Spaniards come from all parts to ask for administrative protection, has given the Madrileño an extraordinary idea of himself, an idea enhanced by triumphs in the national fiesta (football today, not bulls). The most modestly placed man of Madrid scorns the Catalan or Basque millionaire. The word "province" or "provincial" in the mouth of a Madrileño has an incredibly contemptuous ring. It means: pettiness, boredom, gloom.

The truth is that in many respects the proud Madrileño is right. The present government, even more than previous ones, has poured out its protection on the capital. Buildings and parks in Madrid were reborn after the war on an incredibly better scale than in the rest of Spain. Similarly, since it was the city which foreigners preferred to visit, Madrid received permission before any other city to present prohibited plays. On a strange theory of morality which opened the possibility of sinning to residents of Madrid and not to the provinces, for years there were works (Tennessee Williams, for instance) authorized by the censorship for the capital but not for other Spanish cities, even though they might have half a million inhabitants. It is surprising that birth certificates did not have to be shown at the door.

All over the world there is an exodus from the country to the city. In Spain there is also an exodus from the provinces to the capital. Functionaries of all classes suffer in the provinces, dreaming of the longed-for day when they will arrive in Madrid, and the migration of the more ambitious serves to impoverish the life of the provinces and enrich that of the capital. Incorporation in Madrileño life represents a new birth for many provincials, who manage to conceal their regional accent and convert it, if not into a Madrileño style at least into a clear Castilian, and what enchants them most is to hear: "From Galicia? From Catalonia? You've no accent." There is only one exception to those who seek to melt into the Madrileño world, and that is the Andalusians. For them to become Madrileñized is loss, not gain, and all the efforts which other provincials make to hide their original accents, the southerner makes to preserve his.

"Prouder than Don Rodrigo at the gallows."

Spanish pride does not stop in the presence of death, for even death has its categories. It is not the same to be killed by the rope as by the ax; decapitation is reserved for the nobility. When Pedro Crespo, El Alcalde de Zalamea, hangs the captain who has ravished his daughter, the king asks him why, since the offender is a gentleman, he has not ordered him to be beheaded. The mayor answers that the village executioner has not learned to behead because he's had no practice—the nobles of the place are men who give justice no motive for punishing them.

In this connection Spaniards, whether Christian or Moslems, have had the same preoccupation. The social hierarchy extends to death, and even beyond it. The corpse of a king is not the same as that of a soldier. According to Sánchez Albornoz, when Al-Hakam I was getting ready to fight a difficult rebellion in Cordova, he wanted to perfume himself. "Is this a time for perfumes, sire?" a servant asked him. "It is the day on which I must prepare myself for death or victory," replied the Emir, "and I want the head of Al-Hakam to be distinguished from the others who may perish with him."

It has sometimes been said that Spaniards know better how to die than how to live. Especially if there are witnesses. The cases of men who were habitually not very brave and who amazed people by their serenity at the moment of facing the executioner are legion in Spanish history, particularly in the last civil war. Sometimes their attitude is clothed in elegant irony, like that of the man, facing the firing squad, who showed a desire to speak when they were already aiming at him. The officer in charge of the squad delayed the order to fire. Did he want something?

"No, only to warn you that the third gun from the right has a wad in the barrel and some accident might occur."

AVARICE

"He was a pop-gun clergyman, great only in stature . . . each shoe could have been the tomb of a Philistine. And his room? There were not even spiders in it. He exorcised the mice for fear they might nibble some bits of bread he was keeping. He had his bed on the floor and always slept on one side so as not to wear out the sheets. In the end he was arch-poor and proto-miserable."

—QUEVEDO, *La vida del Buscón llamado don Pablos*

"Where there is nobility there is largesse."

THIS chapter will be as short as the previous one was long, and this can be explained. A proud, a haughty, a vain man cannot at the same time be avaricious, mean, or niggardly, for the man who is obliged to keep up appearances shows off first and then counts the pennies, and anyone who thinks it necessary to show off has nothing of Harpagon or Shylock about him.

It is curious that in Spanish literature, nevertheless, there are extraordinary descriptions of misers, such as El Dómine Cabra in *La vida del Buscón llamado don Pablos*, or Torquemada, the great creation of Pérez Galdós. But they are isolated characters compared to the number of hidalgos, students, employees who dress far above their means and invite their friends and acquaintances to dine with them, even at the cost of fasting by themselves later. Among the often-discussed contrasts between Don Quixote and Sancho we do not find meanness. Sancho is as generous as his master when occasion offers, and his anxiety about money and food is only natural in one who has so often seen the cash box and the stomach empty.

Maybe this is why the Spanish people, who are accustomed to use long and often exaggerated words to comment on the defects of others, hardly ever use the word "avaricious" in their descriptions, contenting themselves with "mean," "stingy," "close-fisted" to insult this sin. I say "to insult" because this defect is seldom forgiven in a country where everyone boasts of giving and of their superiority in this respect over other peoples; a popular song says, for example, that St. Martin gave half his cloak to a poor man because he was French; had he been a Spaniard he would have given it all.

But there are few so insulted. When someone has been mentioned in this connection in the circle of my friends, the comment nearly always refers to people who, even though they sometimes hesitate about stretching out their hand for the bill at a restaurant, still dress and treat themselves with singular generosity. In other words, their "avarice" never reaches the extreme of causing them to neglect their food, room, or dress, as would be characteristic of the authentic miser, who is almost as much hurt by the money he spends on keeping up his strength as by what he might spend on entertaining others.

But the Spaniard is generous on a wider scale; with his children, for example, whom he allows to proceed with their studies while he takes additional jobs so that they may be well dressed; or with everyone of his family, whom he supplies with all possible amusements. It is not by chance that Spain has, for instance, one of the highest ratios of cinemas to population in the world and that television now reaches most homes.

The state does well therefore in seeking the greater part of its revenue in indirect taxes levied on shows and restaurants, for few Spaniards hesitate to go to a place because it is above their financial means. (And besides, the other possibility, that of direct taxation or income tax, would have to follow both a change in the Spaniard's idea of the state, as we saw it in the previous chapter, and some way to make him tell the truth about his income, a truth many Spaniards do not even tell their wives.)

"Money is made round so that it may roll."

No, the Spaniard hardly ever sins through avarice. It is possible that in the out-of-the-way mountains there may be, like the village idiot, the village miser, bent on hoarding wealth acquired more or less correctly, but these are isolated cases. The foreigner who comes to Spain is especially astonished at this characteristic of liberality. As Pedro Crespo reminded his son:

> Be polite and agreeable
> be liberal and gay
> for money and doffing your hat
> are what make friends.

The Spaniard shares his lunch with the stranger on the train; after the "May I offer you some?" inherited from the Moors (a gesture which in Spain has a real meaning, as is not the case in other countries) comes the potato tortilla prepared by his wife, or, in the bull ring, the skin of good wine as he fraternizes with whoever happens to be at his side—especially if the neighbor is a foreigner. Among foreigners' memories of Spain there is nearly always the incident on the highway:

"We ran out of gas and had no Spanish money. You know what happened?"

"Yes, a gentleman who was passing stopped, lent you the money and didn't even want to give his address so you could return it."

"How did you know?"

"It happens all the time."

Comparisons are always odious for the one who comes off worse, but without wanting to offend our neighbors I must say that the above does not happen in France or Italy. And the more modest the Spaniard's position, the more earnestly will he insist on your sharing his lunch and his drink, and the more you can offend him if you refuse.

If this generosity were offered only to foreigners, we might explain it by the proud character seen in the previous chapter and put it down to an anxiety to appear well, to do the honors of the house worthily. But the same generosity is exchanged among Spaniards. In no country that I know have I seen less importance given to an invitation by either he who gives it or he who receives it, for they both consider it perfectly natural. When on my first visit to Italy I heard someone say, "He is very kind, he offered us coffee," I was astonished. When has a Spaniard spoken with admiration of such a detail? It would seem natural to him, for he would do exactly the same in the reverse case. And the struggle for the bill in restaurants is in most cases authentic, that is to say it is true that they all want to pay it. And if one of them is slow about it you may be sure he has not the necessary money in his pocket.

Some Spanish proverbs seem to give the lie to this theory of the Spaniard's innate generosity. There is in particular one almost sinister saying: "He who gives bread to someone else's dog loses bread and loses dog." I wish I knew the hidden intention of the man who grumbled like this. What did the wretch want? To keep the bread *and* someone else's dog?

LUST

"One for winning their hearts,
another for bedding them,
one for leaving them,
two for replacing them,
and one hour for forgetting them."

—ZORRILLA's *Don Juan Tenorio*, mentioning the days he
needs for his work (Seventy-two women in one year).

"Who's going to make love to you, gorgeous?"

—*street compliment*

I N Spain lust is in the air. There is nothing clandestine about Spanish appreciation of sex, nothing inhibited, restrained. That is why there are very few sexual crimes in Spain. The man responsible for sexual crimes is usually a puritan who has been warned since childhood against the most serious sins of the flesh. For years he suppresses the desires struggling to come to the surface, and when the explosion occurs his action is as abnormal as has been his restraint. One night, Mr. Smith, the good Mr. Smith with two cats and a dog in his house in Belgrave Square, assaults an old woman and destroys her. Or, like Mr. Christie, walls her up.

This rarely happens in Spain, and not for any lack of the spirit of violence (see Anger). It is just that the pressure to which Mr. Smith has been subject for so many years would be incomprehensible to Juan Pérez, who has been letting off steam all his life, both because he needed to do so and because his society found it normal and logical.

The custom called the *piropo* (flirtation), which foreigners find incredible, is perfectly reasonable to the Spaniard. The *piropo* is the simplest way of letting off steam. It has a wide range of shadings, but fundamentally it is always concrete and comes down to the same thing: the description aloud of a woman's effects on a man, usually followed by the program which the man is prepared to carry out with her.

This declaration of principles is put into effect before an unknown girl who in most cases has not the slightest interest in the *piropeador*. But her indifference has no effect on him, for in delivering his exclamation—ardent, apparently passionate— he is motivated by two governing instincts: one, to purge himself of the desire which seized him at the sight of the girl; the other, to show those around him that he is very much a man and reacts like one at the sight of a woman. Having done so, he can go on talking about football.

(Many foreign ladies who know enough Spanish to understand and be offended by a *piropo* in the street have confessed to me that perhaps the most humiliating thing about a violent declaration by an unknown man is the ease with which he can then be distracted from what he has said.)

"The *piropo*," said Eugenio d'Ors, "is an urgent madrigal"— a definition as inaccurate as it is pretty. As a matter of fact, the *piropo* started as a metaphorical comparison of the oriental type. The Moslem poets of Al Andalus carried their imaginations to extremes when singing to a beloved. If her skin was white: "Never have I seen or heard of such a thing as this, a pearl which from modesty becomes carnelian. So white is her face that when you gaze at its perfections you see your own face submerged in its brightness." Or, "Her lissome waist was a branch that swayed on the sandhill of her hips"; or, "She raised her eyes toward the stars and the stars, admiring so much beauty, got out of their depth and came falling to the cheek where I enviously watched them gutter out."

The extravagant metaphor persists in Spanish songs:

> Your throat, my girl,
> is so lovely and bright
> that the water you drink
> is seen through it.
> My baby's eyes
> are of new bread
> and mine are dying
> of hunger.

It would be pleasant if *piropos* went on like this.

Unfortunately, with things as they are, the tiny minority capable of such imagery, the authentic poets, are rather timid, so the streets remain in the hands of two groups: those who roar out the previously mentioned program of possible pleasures and those who, limited by lack of imagination, repeat a thousand and one times what the old poets wrote ("Your eyes are bigger than your feet," and so on). There is a third group which says feebly, "Olé, the pretty woman! Yes sir!" or "That's the way to walk!"

Spanish humorists have had great fun with this phenomenon.

Fernández Flórez in *Relato Inmoral* describes a Spaniard educated abroad and therefore with little experience of the *piropo*. When the urging of his friends forces him to follow a girl in the street, he does so in troubled silence, until the "Long live your mother, you glorious darling" recommended by his mentors becomes a polite and timid "Señorita, I desire long life for your lady mother."

"A girl pulls more than a rope."

The worst thing about the *piropo* is the obligation to give it. Spanish males reason more or less as follows: I am very much a man. It is therefore natural that a woman who goes by should produce a reaction of desire in me. And logically I ought to express it aloud so that she may know about it.

Often, he is the one who has to know about it.

We Spaniards learn from childhood how important it is to flaunt our maleness, to show how far removed we are from femininity. All of a boy's gestures, his words, and naturally his voice have to reflect this position continually, if he is not to provoke the ridicule of his companions.[1] When I was adolescent one could not smoke with the right hand, because it was considered effeminate. (In the play *Usted tiene ojos de mujer fatal,* Jardiel says of a lady, "The only difference between her and a carabineer was that she smoked with the right hand.") I did not understand then—nor do I now—the mysterious connection between raising a cigarette to one's mouth with the right hand and femininity. But I was naturally very careful not to challenge the taboo of society. Today I do not smoke, but if I did, I would hold the cigarette in my left hand. Of course!

The need for a continual display of manliness affects other activities—work, for instance. For a long time stevedores and

---

[1] Perhaps this is why the Spanish homosexual raises his voice and exaggerates his gestures more than his French, Italian, or English counterpart. He has to go farther to get "to the other side."

construction men refused to wear protective gloves. "That," they said, "is for sissies."

The magic circle the Spaniard traces around his virility is as clear-cut as are most of his beliefs. A man, just because he is one, can see beauty *only* in a woman. When a girl asks a Spaniard about the physical aspect of some boy, he is sure to say "I don't see these things in men." That is to say, he cannot notice the perfection of the boy's nose or the size of his eyes or whether he has good teeth. He flatly refuses to comment or judge, and we deduce from his reply that he could not distinguish between Paul Newman and Quasimodo. "I don't see these things in men."

When he is obliged by the nature of some story to describe a good-looking man, the most he will say is that he has "a good appearance," a vague description which does not compromise him as would—God preserve us!—"He is handsome." After all, in the lustful imagination of the Spaniard all physical admiration is irrevocably attached to one object; his subconscious, in terror, rejects the possibility of being attracted to his own sex.

Another thing a real man evidently cannot sense in another— the same thing occurs with women—is that special quality with which people even of insignificant appearance can conquer the opposite sex. The "it," the sex appeal. (And note the phrase "I don't know what you see in her," the typical remark of a beautiful woman referring to one who is plain but irresistible to men.)

Virility is protected with great care all through a Spaniard's life; a Spanish man seriously compromises himself as a male if he does such womanly things as carry a parcel of sweets along the street—parcels in general, and especially flowers. A man with a bunch of carnations in his hand is laughable, and it is one of our paradoxes that the only man who walks and even salutes with flowers is the bravest and most virile of Spaniards, the matador.

Naturally a Spaniard does not go near the kitchen, which he considers quite outside his sphere of action. He may at times, as a favor, prepare a dish which requires intelligence and elegance (a *paella*, for instance). But this is a special occasion, and he will never stay in the kitchen afterward to clean up. This would gravely compromise his prestige, and the women support this notion by expelling from their domains any man who dares propose to help them. "But no, this is no place for men!" a married Spanish lady said to me in California, astonished at American customs. "I prefer to do it myself, even if I am ill. See my husband in an apron?—But no, no!"

But the guarding of virility in public—which seems to be the important thing, given the importance of *qué dirán*—has greater obligations. The Spaniard dresses in a way which leaves no room for doubts as to his sex. His suits are dark, his ties have hardly a note of color, his tailoring is as little exaggerated as possible. Still, his instinct for elegance makes him want to follow the fashions, so there is in his taste for dress a constant inner struggle which can only be eased with time. For example, a man approaches, wearing a brightly colored beach shirt; it provokes exclamations of astonishment if the wearer is a friend, smiles and nudges if he is a stranger. "Have you seen how that boy's got up, what a scream!"

This will last perhaps a year. Little by little the fashion takes over, is accepted. To most people it is no longer effeminate. Those who mocked before now wear colored shirts while walking along the same street which was the scene of their former amazement. Now they are surprised at a foreigner whose trousers are shorter than the normal. "But have you seen, what a scream how he's got up? I'm telling you, he's lost all shame. . . ." Until the following year.

Again, the curious thing is that the bravest and most virile of Spaniards, the matador, dresses "like a woman," in silks, bright colors. This anomaly inspired Fernández Flórez years ago to propose an interesting theory, according to which the matador is a symbol of sexual love. The matador—narrow-waisted, graceful in his movements—is the woman. The bull—brutal, direct, following only instinct—is the man. The female symbol moves before him, provokes him with its body and gestures, makes him jealous (*encelar*, to make jealous, is used even by bullfight critics); when the bull attacks it finds itself frustrated and turns against its enemy, more furious than ever. Just as in coquetry. The matador triumphs at the end, and in the death-possession there is always blood. This victory, then, may be a symbol of woman's dominion over man, since Adam and Eve, Omphale and Hercules. In some cases—they are few—the balance has come down on the other side, that is to say with the defeat of the tormentor, the woman.

The obsession about not appearing effeminate naturally produces, when coupled with dislike for someone (see Envy), an easily made accusation: "They tell me that . . ." Up to a few years ago this accusation could be effectively rebutted with a declaration of civil status: "No, man, how can he be that when he's married and has children?" Today this is not enough to silence slander. "That doesn't matter in the least. He likes both sexes." Thus, there is practically no way to rebut the accusation—how can a person be proved *not* to be homosexual if being heterosexual does not preclude the possibility?

The Spaniard sallies out into the street every morning prepared to demonstrate to the world how masculine he is. The *piropo* is his prerequisite, the banner unfurled to the wind to show his psychological equilibrium as a perfect man, always ready to attack. The women he meets have to suffer—that's what women are for, O Lord!—suffer that fire which burns within him, if not the flame at least the sparks, and to accept this demonstration of his self-consuming ardor.

Spanish sexual aggressiveness is traditional, and while the subject is generally absent in books and plays, the history of the country tells of a prince who died of his excesses. He was Juan, the son of the Catholic King Ferdinand and Queen Isabella. Married very young to Margaret of Burgundy, he embarked upon conjugal life with such ardor that the doctors recommended that the newly married pair separate for a time to give the prince a chance to recuperate. Queen Isabella, it seems, answered that she could not separate those whom God had joined together, even for a reason of state, and the prince died within a few months. It appears evident that the blame for

what happened fell largely on the bride, to whose temperament
we have an interesting reference: When Margaret was still a
child she had been married by proxy to a French prince. The
marriage was annulled before she had time even to see her
betrothed. For political reasons, and again by proxy, she later
married Prince Juan, and on her voyage to Spain a storm
threatened to sink both the ship and her illusions. In order that
her body should be recognized if the sea should cast her on the
shore, the princess wrote some lines on a piece of wood tied to
her wrist:

> Ici git Margot, la gentille demoiselle
> deux fois mariée et morte pucelle.
> (Here lies Margaret, the gentle damsel,
> who was twice married and died a virgin.)

Sensuality is in the Spaniard's lips and glance, and continually in his conversation; but, a curious fact, it seldom
appears in his books. Detailed description of sexual matters can
hardly be found in Spanish literature, and the blame for this
should not be laid only on the Inquisition, which was much less
strict in this regard than the present censorship. It seems that
the Spaniard resents the idea of revealing sexual sentiments.
There remain some descriptions of the figure of a medieval lady:
"Her tiny titties want to burst her silken dress," or the delight
of possession as recounted in *La Celestina*, or the charming
shamelessness of the love scenes in Francisco Delicado's *La
lozana andaluza*, crude rather than pornographic. Perhaps, as
an island, Góngora's sonnet:

> . . . A humor among the pearls distilled
> and which the sacred liquor need not envy
> the boy of Ida served to Jupiter. . . .

. . . but even here there is an attempt to discourage the reader
from indulgence:

> Lovers, do not touch if you want to live
> for in between one red lip and another
> there abides love, arméd with his poison
> like hidden serpent betwixt flower and flower. . . .

And at the end:

> All that is left of love is the poison.

Sexual love is restricted by public and private morality, and by religion. For the Catholic Spaniard, the sexual act incurs some punishment, be it the violent death of Calixto and Melibea in *La Celestina* or simply the disillusionment which follows the enjoyment.

This would not naturally occur to those Spaniards who follow the comfortable and understanding religion of Mohammed. Four legitimate wives, all the concubines one can support, and if one dies in combat, the ascent to a paradise with black-eyed houris attending to one's needs.

And though frowned upon, indulgence in another sensual pleasure, that of wine, was not forbidden by the Prophet. It was as much appreciated by the Andalusians of that time as by those of today, as in this eleventh-century account:

> When full of drunkenness she fell asleep and the eyes
> of the night patrol fell asleep
> . . . I approached her timidly like a friend who seeks
> furtive contact feigningly
> I approached her insensibly like sleep; I rose toward
> her sweetly as breath.
> I kissed the bright whiteness of her neck; I drained
> the lively redness of her mouth.
> And I spent my night deliciously with her until the
> darkness smiled, showing the white teeth of the dawn.

The sight of an unusually exposed girl both exhilarates and irritates the Spaniard. He follows her with his gaze, and even with his steps if they happen to be going the same way, but he vacillates between *piropos* and curses on her impudence. It seems that custom has laid down the maximum amount of flesh that a girl may offer to a Spaniard's eyes. If there is one inch more, it seems to him an insulting provocation, a mocking challenge. With his natural inclination to see everything as part of his own world, he finds in this exhibition not a strange taste or fashion but a deliberate intention to mortify him:

"They've no right, man, they've no right! You can't go through the streets like that! They ought to be killed!"

Spanish women usually display what they should and no more, and Spanish men marvel at certain photographs from Paris. How is it possible for these women to expose themselves without people assaulting the stage? What's wrong with the Frenchmen? It is in vain to explain that the same proportion between male desire and customs of female exposure exists for all countries and throughout time, that today's Frenchmen are as normal as our own fathers, who were excited at the sight of an ankle. For the Spaniard, who lives in the immediate present, this is no explanation. In his heart he prefers to believe that Frenchmen are simply not made as he is. They haven't the same blood, for heaven's sake!

Now the Spaniard, *he*, of course, is heir to an irresistible Donjuanesque tradition. His manners are good, he talks well, he is romantic and sexually powerful. How could women not fall down before him?

I believe every Spaniard is really a potential Don Juan. He is a polygamist *par excellence* and, possibly, in general more competent at physical love than men in other countries. In my opinion there are good reasons for this: First, he spends much of his time commenting on the sexual act, and his descriptions tend to keep him in a state of excitement; second, and perhaps more important, his working hours, as we know, are far shorter than those of other Europeans and of North Americans. It is obvious that a man submitted to less pressure of business and decision-making, one who adds a siesta to eight hours' sleep a night, is much better prepared for adventure. A third reason might be the intelligent use the Spaniard makes of alcohol, to which I referred earlier. As the drunken porter in *Macbeth* says of wine: "Lechery, sir, it provokes, and unprovokes; it provokes the desire, but it takes away the performance." Shakespeare knew his countrymen when he wrote this warning.

But the most Donjuanesque characteristic of the Spaniards, as I see it, is the one we find in Tenorio, so important that without it we cannot understand the type. It is the *relating* of one's exploits, a thing so basic that it often seems their exclusive motivation. In the opening scenes of Zorrilla's work, Don Juan and Don Luis (a Don Juan with worse luck) take obvious pleasure in narrating the history of the year:

> That was a deed, by heaven!
> Those are the ones that bring fame!
>
> While Seville reposes
> believing me imprisoned
> I add two more names
> to my numerous list.

It is vital that their exploits be known, and from this fact springs Marañón's well-known theory denying the supermasculinity of a man who continually needs to prove it.

There is a story going around Spain of a doctor in a provincial capital who, in amazement and wonder, received an offer of love from the most beautiful and distinguished lady in the city. His joy turned to sadness, however, when she put one condition on their intimate relations: that nobody should know about them.

"You mean I can't tell about it at the club?" the doctor is said to have replied. "Then I'm not interested."

It is only with reluctance that Spaniards accept the entry of women into clubs and cafés; they prefer to be alone among men—so that they can talk about women. The descriptions, narratives, details of sexual contact are analyzed, studied, discussed with scientific eagerness. The fact that Spanish men usually don't marry until they are nearly thirty allows them time to have many experiences to recount.

If a man is married, he does not describe the intimate details of his relationship with his wife, which is sacred. He either keeps his mouth shut when the rest describe their exploits or tells of extramarital adventures, which naturally need not be veiled.

When the Spaniard encounters a difficulty imposed by the state or the Church, his instinct leads him to circumvent it. There is no divorce in Spain, but there are certainly many couples living in concubinage. (This word is never used in Spain as it sounds too strong, far beyond the way the affair appears to people. It sounds better to say "He has a girlfriend" or "She has a man-friend." This appropriation of such a common term makes it virtually useless when referring to a non-sexual relationship.)

In Spain, a man generally sees women as divided into two wholly different and separate groups. In one are his mother, his sisters, and his wife; in the other, prostitutes. There is an enormous gulf between their two worlds. "My wife on an altar," the husband feels, even before going out on the town: the wife, at home with the children, is the moral reserve on which he must draw from time to time to purify himself. The other thing is an adventure, which if necessary he can put in the dimunitive form: *"aventurilla"* sounds better, because for the man it "has no importance." For the woman it is anything but a little adventure. It is adultery.

In *Miguel Rivera*, Palacio Valdés gives us a fascinating dialogue:

> "Ay, Miguel! How did you dare kiss a married woman? Aren't you afraid God will punish you?"
> The young man's face darkened suddenly. A deep, perverse furrow appeared in his brow and he remained thoughtful for a while. At last in a hoarse voice, gazing into the fire, Miguel said:
> "If a thing like that happened to me and I found out about it, I know what I should have to do. The first thing would be to put my wife into the street, day or night, at whatever time I learned about it. . . ."

Miguel judges very differently what might be done to him and what he is accustomed to do to others, but at least he makes an effort to put himself in the other's shoes. Most Spaniards who try to conquer a woman never think of her husband's rights, or her brother's feelings, because (as we saw in Pride) they are incapable of seeing from another's point of view. A Spaniard may spend months convincing a girl to forget what she has been taught about morals and religion, but he would be tremendously annoyed if his sister surrendered to another man the smallest liberty that he hopes to obtain from his girlfriend.

When the Spaniard walks in the streets with his wife, fiancée, or sister, he looks suspiciously and sternly at all passing males. Anyone who steals a glance at the señora or señorita will doubtless encounter—if he shifts his glance a few inches—unfriendly eyes: "What are you looking at, man? You ought to be ashamed of yourself!" When the same Spaniard is walking alone he looks at women with the impudence he disapproved of previously. I have never heard a Spaniard allow his sister to hear—with the same reason and right—the coarse remarks he says to someone else's sister. "Why?" I have asked. "What do you mean, why?" they have answered, indignant at my lack of understanding. "It's very different!" Of course, completely different; it's a question of someone else.

In their own, highly personal interpretation of the divine laws, Spanish men generally maintain that they may do what is forbidden to Spanish women. Not even the curious precision with which the commandment says "Thou shalt not covet thy neighbor's wife," without even mentioning that the wife should not covet her neighbor's husband,[1] calms the Spaniard's polygamous zeal. His eagerness for another man's wife is so great that the same individual who might hesitate about marrying a widow, because he would not be the first, presumes on the other hand to enjoy intimate relations with a woman who has cuckolded her husband for him. Maybe he sees in this second case a gallant proof of a battle won, and in the other only a more or less humiliating inheritance.

> *"If in the Canonical Decrees there is no remission,*
> *who'll have the luck to enter into glory?"*

The idea behind the proverb seems more ironical than forbidding. Given the great number of sinners, it appears clear that an amnesty will be granted, such as the state offers when

[1] Perhaps the Spaniard's instinctive distrust of others explains the unpleasant double meaning of the word *prójima*: literally "neighbor," the feminine form usually means "whore."

those who neglect to pay their debts are too numerous to be put in prison.

Most Spanish women consider the paradoxes of the double standard natural. They have been told since they were children that the physical needs of men are greater than their own and that the man's sin is therefore more logical. "Men, as you know . . ." they say. "What did you do when you found out that Papa was deceiving you?" is the casual question asked by a daughter in a contemporary play, as if the situation were perfectly normal.

When wives leave their husbands to go on vacation with their children, a very normal occurrence in Spain, the husband remains alone and abandoned to his luck in the great city full of enchantments. The wife often considers it natural that he cannot remain faithful for so many weeks and, though she will not call him to account, only trusts he will not fall into the hands of someone who will exploit his weakness. (Most Spanish women I have questioned on this subject, asking them what confidence they have in their husbands, have refused with the same energy (a) to believe that their husband deceives them, and (b) to swear that he never has.)

Does this tradition perhaps go back to the Arabs? The official certificate a married woman had to sign in Moslem Spain read: "So-and-so, daughter of So-and-so, calls for irrefutable evidence against her from the witnesses mentioned in this document, that her husband So-and-so, son of So-and-so, has asked her permission to keep a concubine . . . and the wife permits him to do so, authorizing him to have a concubine . . . a thing which she does voluntarily and with pleasure."

The before-mentioned distinction between decent and indecent women is directly applied to all Spanish circumstances and customs. Any woman who does not adjust herself strictly to these is relegated automatically to the other side of the dividing line. In the rigid Spanish mind, a decent woman does some things in public and does not do others. For our grandparents, a woman was indecent who "smoked and called men *tu*," or used make-up, or showed her knees. With fashions, as we have seen when speaking of virility, the first impact of change is always regarded with suspicion.

"If you're not selling it, cover it up."

The saying might have a certain logic with reference to the generosity of the exhibition, because it used to be that women who showed a centimeter more bosom or leg than was customary were indeed interested in selling those goods, but the principle is more complicated. An Italian woman journalist who was in Spain in 1947 dared to appear in a dress by Dior, who at that time had just *lengthened* the skirt. She produced in the Madrid of those days laughter, scornful comments, sarcastic whistles. But what puzzled her most was the cry of a woman who pointed accusingly at her in the entrance of a subway station: "Indecent! Indecent!"

The false Spanish syllogism that decent women cover themselves as far as here, this woman covers herself less, therefore this woman is not decent, is applied unreservedly without thought of national origin. Therefore most foreign women who arrive in Spain with different jewelry and make-up are automatically placed in the category of the easy-to-gets. "Just look how she's dressed, she must be common. . . . And what's more she's traveling alone. . . . We all know that a woman who travels alone or with a girl friend . . . We all know that abroad . . ."

The Spaniard thereupon hastens to the conquest, and often achieves it. His expressions are ardent, his gestures romantic, his allusions to the stars opportune, and usually he has time to devote to his enterprise. The Donjuanesque legend of romantic Spain is in his favor, and so is the idea of many women that a journey is a parenthesis in life and that inhibitions stay at home with the family.

At other times, the conquest may leave him with a bitter sense of failure—through his own fault. His society has taught him that decent and indecent women are differentiated not only by the purity of the former and the impurity of the latter, but also in a profound social sense. An indecent woman not only acts permissively in her intimate life; she is also common, vulgar, provocative, and in general quite the opposite of a lady in her gestures and manner. The Spaniard in dealing with such a woman employs his worst vocabulary, talks to her "as if he were among men."

Hence his surprise when he meets the strange type of foreign woman who accepts his caresses while maintaining, both before and after, an incredible dignity ("as if nothing had happened between us, can you imagine it?"), and who furthermore demands that she be treated as a lady. Some men have imagined they are being made fun of and have reacted so violently as to lose all possibilities for the future, to their great astonishment. After all, if she does it once . . .

This first time is very important for the Spaniard. A whole folklore exists to explain the gravity of the first time, which can be likened to flinging oneself down from a precipice. The popular songs of years ago, like the romantic dramas, and even older works, show that for the woman who once gives herself outside legitimate marriage there is no path but prostitution, and the bad man who started her on it appears in all the tales of "ladies of the town."

> That man who was the ingrate
> who mocked my love one day
> and before long forgot
> what he had promised before;
> I placed myself before him,
> panting with rage, and told him
> my evil life.

For without reputation, women cannot live normal lives. They had their honor and it was taken from them. The verb *deshonrar* has a harsh connotation that is completely Spanish.

A train is going through the fields of Aragon. In a third-class compartment there are two people, a man and a woman: they are peasants and have just got married; they are on their honeymoon. The train is jolting, the woman wrapped in her shawl is shivering with cold and embarrassment—it is the first time she has been alone with a man. He, motionless, in front of her with his greatcoat up to his neck and his cap pulled over his eyes, is silent too. The hard seat jerks about, the wind from the Moncayo whistles through the badly closed windows. Two hours pass in silence. And finally he says in a hoarse voice, "Do I dishonor you here or in Calatayud?"

Obviously this is an extreme case even in Spain. No inhabitant of Madrid or Barcelona or any other important city would say such a thing. But it is symbolic. Honor . . . When a woman loses it there is an explosion. The sin, like a stone tied around her neck, plunges the sinner deeper, deeper. She cannot now check herself down the path of sin. A woman who has been with a man is easy prey.

In one of his most ironic stories, *Relato inmoral*, Fernández Flórez describes the case of the traditional jealous fiancé who succeeds in obtaining the favors of his future wife twenty-four hours before the wedding—and then abandons her as unworthy. How is he going to trust someone who gave herself to a man who was not yet her husband?

The same scruples apply to virginity as to marital honor. And it is just as serious if virginity is presumed lost as if it has in fact been lost. The act is important in itself, but not so important as its publication. This explains something in our literature which is incomprehensible from a realistic standpoint, the ease with which the characters in the classical plays and novels achieve their lustful goals after entering a young lady's room. The difficulty, it seems, is getting in, what with locked doors, watchful servants, and especially the fathers, always on the lookout to see that no one should stain the family coat of arms. The bold overcome these material barriers by various means: killing or bribing the maid, breaking down the door, or deceiving the master of the house by posing as a teacher of music or some other specialty, or, in his absence, by obtaining a counterfeit key. But once they manage to get in with one means or another, the rest is extremely easy. The woman may be an accomplice who waits for him or she may be taken by surprise; the result is the same. The man enjoys her.

"And when my maiden turned to leave the room, I was no longer one," says Dorotea in *Quixote*, in the briefest and most summary of confessions. In this case she accepted his coming beforehand, but the same thing would have happened if she had opposed him. There is hardly a single case in classical literature in which the woman resists, screams, or throws the intruder out of her room. The man triumphs even when she is waiting for another man. This is the case with Zorrilla's Don Juan, who obtains Doña Ana, the fiancée of Don Luis; the latter complains as follows:

> You have handcuffed me
> and assaulted the house
> usurping my place!
> And as you took mine
> to triumph over Doña Ana
> it is not you, Don Juan, who wins,
> since you were playing for another.

How, even in the darkness, Doña Ana was unable to distinguish Don Juan from Don Luis is difficult to explain. The duchess in Tirso's *El Burlador* did not notice any difference between her Octavio and Don Juan, either. It seems clear on the whole that the woman's reaction on seeing a man in her room is always the same: her honor is already blemished. Nobody could think anything but the worst, anyway, and if she is going to be despised in any case . . .

Things reached such a point that for a long time to "dishonor" meant both the physical act and speaking ill of a woman. In Cervantes' sketch "La Guarda cuidadosa," the maid says to her master and mistress that the sacristan dishonored her in the middle of the street, which terrifies those whose obligation it was to protect her. It turns out later that he merely insulted her in public.

The importance of virginity in Spain comes both from its Christian tradition (the Virgin Mary) and from the Moslem one. In the matrimonial laws of the eleventh century, it was laid down that a father had to "cover himself" legally for his daughter's accidental loss of her maidenhead by making the following statement: "So-and-so, son of So-and-so, calls for proof that it has been the purpose of Allah (may he be honored and exalted) that his daughter So-and-so, a virgin under his jurisdiction, by falling from a stair, from a ladder or by falling onto such and such a thing, should lose her maidenhead, which is revealed by her father So-and-so when she is still below the age of puberty, at the time when this evidence is attested, in order that it may be public and well known among the people, thus avoiding the moral degradation of his daughter and so that when she reaches puberty no one shall believe more than what is said in this document to have happened, and whoever shall believe anything else and impute it to So-and-so and defame her will be sinning. . . . They give evidence of what has been put upon record in this document. . . ."

The almost superstitious veneration for virginity and the consequent contempt for the spinster who loses it produce curious reactions.

I have often been the confidant of Spaniards who have gone abroad for the first time and have suffered a tremendous shock (Spain has been shut up in herself for a long time) on breathing different air. I have heard more than one become indignant at the "no" of a German or English woman whom he knew had had a relationship with another man.

"Just imagine! That kind of stuff to me—when I know she's been so-and-so's lover."

My answer surprised them much more.

"And What's-his-name's . . . and You-know-who's . . . and a hundred others you don't know, but not yours, you see how strange she is. . . ."

He could not believe it. All the easy women he had known in Spain were so because, having fallen once, they had fallen forever. From the love of one they had passed to the love of all, supported by the certainty that no man would have accepted them as the only one. The fact that there should exist women who are not ashamed of such a past, who allow themselves the luxury of choosing those who accompany them to their room, fills the Spaniard with amazement and sometimes with spite.

Such a disappointment represents, besides, a failure in his plans for the trip abroad. The Spaniard is generally certain that on the other side of the Pyrenees he will encounter paradise (not the Christian but the Moslem one, with houris at hand). The freedom of foreign custom is the object of comment in schools and colleges, and hardly has the entry visa for another country been stamped in the Spaniard's passport than he stretches out his neck in search of the adventure that must await him at the first station. Often he finds it—thanks to his persistent searching—but on many occasions he fails, owing to his precipitation and brusqueness in asking the question. In her own setting, and with her own problem of *qué dirán*, the foreign woman wants to be persuaded, not snatched up.

When his hopes are cut short, when the reality does not live up to his expectations, the Spaniard reacts characteristically. If the reality "fails," he changes it. The Spaniard who had no adventures invents them exactly "as they should have occurred." I remember a friend's confession in Venice: "When I left you last night, something happened to me. . . ." (It always happens when you are not there.) "I went to the hotel bar and had a drink before turning in. And suddenly, my boy, there was a gorgeous woman who kept looking at me. I was sleepy. . . . I had my drink and went to my room. I'd just put on my pajamas and lit a cigarette when there was a knock at the door—"

"—And it was the lady from the bar."

"Quite right. She begged my pardon, wanted to know if I had a match—just imagine. . . ." (He had done all he could to help me in this operation, obviously.)

Then he thought it over a little. The adventure as he had described it appeared too common. He added, "I tell you, she comes from a very good family."

I have heard this story situated in New York, Paris, Berlin, London, and Hong Kong. There are variants (instead of a hotel room it may be a cabin on a ship, or a sleeper on a train, the girl may ask for a glass of water or an aspirin), but there are always three indispensible features. First the extraordinary beauty of the woman, second the initial indifference of the man (the initiative always comes from her), third the high social class of the intruder, who may attain titled rank.

This threefold coincidence is of course what makes me skeptical about these stories, which as I see them correspond to what the men hoped would happen when they first went abroad. (Maybe my suspicion is due to resentment, for nothing like this has ever happened to me on visits to fifty countries.)

The Spaniard lives with, for, in, and by lust. The sexual organs acquire in Spain, apart from their normal nomenclature, an infinite variety of names, many of which are completely at variance with the laws of logic. (There is a familiar noun for the male organ which is feminine, and vice versa.) Any verbal stumble by an ignorant foreigner against these idioms produces roars of laughter and winks among those present; the nature of the countryside, the shape of roads, and so forth are continually studied for possible new expressions.

One energetic statement used by the Spaniard insists that he does something or stops doing it because "it comes from my balls." Usually it is a matter of an action which has no reason to spring from such an unexpected source.

There is a statue in Madrid (in Alcalá, opposite the Retiro) of a general of whom most people know very little. They have all, however, given sufficient attention to a certain part of the horse's anatomy to be able to use it as a point of reference: "as big as . . . , bigger than . . ."

For every Spaniard, going out into the street represents the chance of an erotic adventure. He moves in full stride like a combatant on the field of battle, and anyone standing in a crowded subway car with a nice-looking girl amid the mass may observe a whole range of illusions, hopes, and desires in the faces of those surrounding her, from the distant one who cranes his neck and tries to slip closer, to those beside her who press against her as much as possible while their eyes wander over the advertisements on the windows. It is a silent combat in which the girl defends herself as she can, trying to differentiate the casual contact from the malicious, the involuntary shove from the deliberate. Heels on the male shoe, elbowings, and at times a pin are her usual weapons, and the battle develops in impressive silence while the train passes several stations. When the victim departs at her destination, the persecutors are left looking at one another as if lost, as if a tremendous abyss had suddenly opened before their feet.

This constant presence of sex in the Spanish streets produces a constant defense against it. Eyes fixed on the ground, a grave expression on her face, the girl who wants to avoid giving the importunate man a chance is a guarded soul. She lives in such apprehension of what a man may attempt against her that she normally will not even answer a stranger who asks her a direction, which astonishes and puzzles the lost foreigner.

Even when she is not alone, she has to take protective measures. If a couple arrives at the cinema, and beside the seat which the girl would normally take there is a fairly young man, her escort will occupy this seat and leave her outside, next to the aisle if possible. The operation is carried out without any pretence—"No, you sit here"—while he stares at the suspicious character. This impertinence is nearly always passed over in silence, as if the one alluded to had really seen his plot exposed. And in general it is true that Spanish girls do not use the armrest between their seat and their neighbor's, and will sit well back so as to give no incitement to explorations and skirmishing. As for the man, any activity will be based (a) on a man's normal reaction, and (b) on the fear that if he does not try, at least try, the girl's judgment will be contemptuous.

Fathers of families are well aware of this danger and arrange their daughters' places carefully, so that they are hemmed in by themselves and a brother, however small he may be. If in spite of these precautions fate wills that a girl have a flank uncovered, the good gentleman will not hesitate to look around from time to time and cast an inquisitive warning glance at any man in the seat of opportunity: "Be very careful." A friend of mine told me in horror that in such cases her father said every now and then, "Is that gentleman molesting you, my dear. Tell me—is he molesting you?" while she shrugged her shoulders in denial and the other man gazed steadily at the screen as if he was a thousand miles from the apocalyptic voice.

A character in Lope de Vega's *Los Vargas de castilla* complains about this family vigilance:

> How tedious is honor—
> I am bored by what is good for me!
> They mustn't look at me, or see me
> or whisper to me or talk
> or think of me when they pass.
> Jesus, So-and-so saw me!
> Shut the door, oh dear!
> If I mention that I saw him?
> No, I watched him before.
> If my father heard about it,
> if our neighbor saw him,
> if it were noticed in the street,
> if my brother knew about it . . .
> my reputation, my honor,
> my blood, my social position,
> my being and my honesty . . .
> Can there be anything worse?

*"Between the male and female saints
there must be a stone wall."*

The Spaniard sees the sexual act as the basis and symbol of any prolonged relationship between man and woman. It is not only that he doesn't believe in platonic friendship between a man and woman; he does not even accept a close friendship between man and man, or woman and woman, without very soon imputing to it a sexual hue. In Spain, I always warn my American girls studying Spanish, you cannot say "my friend told me"; you must say "a friend of mine told me." Why? Because if only one friend is mentioned, Spaniards will automatically think it is a lover. But why? Oh, because that's how

it is. And can't you say "my friend" using the feminine form?
Not that, either.

This obsession with seeing any two persons who come near
each other as potential sexual partners leads to a violent reaction to acts which in other countries would pass as signs of
normal affection. For years, especially in small villages, a kiss
on the movie screen has produced an explosion of shouting,
whinnying, and phrases auguring greater pleasure. Foreign
couples who say goodbye affectionately in a public place in
Spain have found themselves surrounded by faces showing a
mixture of irony and lewdness. For the Spaniard, the kiss is the
gateway that leads to all the rest, and more than one American
girl (who may kiss as easily as she combs her hair) has found
her goodbye to a Spaniard transformed into a ten-minute
struggle, until the other has realized that the kiss was not the
aperitif but the dessert.

The present government could have solved this problem
gradually by accustoming the Spanish people to the expressions
of affection used in America and in the rest of the European
world. But impelled by a strict morality, it took a different
course, that of censoring love scenes from movies. For many
years (this has changed recently) the audience would see a man
and a woman approaching each other with open arms—only to
find them already moving away in the following shots. This
greatly angered the public, deprived of a tidbit which it
imagined, like anything forbidden, to be much more substantial
than it actually was.

But sometimes cutting was not enough, for the "evil" went
deeper; the immorality lay in a situation rather than in one
scene, and cutting it all would kill the film, depriving the public
of another possibility of amusement. (As in nearly all poor
countries, the cinema represents a delicious escape both in a
visual way—beauty, luxury, exotic landscapes—and in a material sense: for many Spaniards who live in old houses, the
cinema means soft seats, warmth in winter and air-conditioning
in summer.) So another solution was sought, whereby the theme
of the film should reach the spectator in a different form from

what the writer and director had intended. For this the censors employed a powerful weapon, dubbing, which is now used in Spain with the great majority of foreign films. It no longer mattered what the characters originally said in French, English, or German, as they were going to say something else in Spanish.

People began not to understand anything of the films they were shown. I remember a famous one with Margaret Sullavan and Charles Boyer. The latter played a married man in love with a spinster. He could not fulfill his dream as his wife refused to grant him a divorce, so the three of them went on, gradually getting older, in a tense situation which was complicated and aggravated by the reaction of the children on discovering their father's secret.

The censorship decided that this plot was most immoral and transformed the dialogue so as to arrive at the following situation: the character played by Charles Boyer was a bachelor who lived with his widowed sister and his nephews and nieces. Throughout the film, whenever his beloved asked him sorrowfully, "Why don't we get married?" he answered, lowering his head, "My sister doesn't want us to—she will never give her consent. . . ."

The audience came out highly astonished, but the possibility of deceit was rejected as unbelievable. They preferred to think patriotically that "those Americans are weak in the head."

An even more awkward case occurred in a more recent film, *Mogambo*. Grace Kelly was the wife of a hunter and Clark Gable the head of the safari. The flirtation between Grace Kelly and Clark Gable had little importance for the audience because the lady was not married (in spite of the ring which could not be dubbed out); her companion was simply her brother. And why, as he was her brother, did he seem so upset by the meetings of the lovers? It was a difficult problem, but the censor solved it in his own way. Taking advantage of a moment when Grace Kelly was looking away from the camera, the dubbing man had her say hurriedly, "My brother does not look with favor on our relationship because he's a close friend of my fiancé, who is ill in a hospital in London."

Of course it was an explanation, though even so the attitude seemed highly exaggerated, but what puzzled the audience most was the fact that the brother and sister always shared the same room and tent. For evil thinkers, the moral turned out even more damaging in the expurgated version.

When Spaniards started to travel—few of them did so before 1950—and told on their return about the films they had seen abroad, the popular imagination overflowed. In every scene that was cut the audience believed they could see the censor's scissors depriving them of endless embraces or at least of the physical charms of the actress in her bedroom or bathroom. "Did you see *Gilda* abroad?" I was once asked. "What luck! Here they cut it out in the most ghastly way. You remember when Rita Hayworth was going to dance and took off her gloves, beginning at the elbow? Well, here they cut it out after that."

"And that," I replied, "is the end of the scene."

"What? Didn't she take all her clothes off?"

The obsession became a joke. "You know that scene in *Marabunta* where there are thousands of ants advancing through the forest? Well, in the version they show in Paris, instead of ants they're naked women."

Films are censored everywhere, but apart from the fact that this does not console the Spaniard, who hates following rules ("evil of many, consolation of fools"), the censorship causes more irritation in Spain than elsewhere because it does not correspond to the sociological reality, whereas in other countries official morality is more likely to coincide with private morality. In Catholic Ireland, for instance, everyone agrees that one should not eat meat on Fridays in Lent, and the state's stricture against serving it reflects the ideas of individuals. On the other hand, in France the nakedness of an actress does not upset anyone who has seen the same thing on the covers of hundreds of magazines in any bookstall.

But in Spain, official morality is infinitely stricter than private morality. The censorship decides that here neither adultery nor premarital relations nor homosexuality exists, and as they do not exist it is useless and dangerous to open the eyes of Spaniards to these excesses. But as the spectator knows that the lady next door receives a married man, and remembers that some distant cousins of his had to get married, and has heard that So-and-so is queer, he resents this excessive protection which treats him like a stupid child, incapable of seeing life as it is.

Film directors and especially playwrights have often heard the same warning. "In Spain these things do not occur. If you wish to touch on these subjects, situate the action in a foreign country, in France, for instance, because we all know there is plenty of vice there." On one occasion, Alfonso Paso had to transform the setting of a comedy based on the traditional story of *The Rodríguez*. "Rodríguez" is the name (corresponding to "Smith" in English) given by lone husbands who stay in Madrid during the summer to the girls who also stay behind in order to console their loneliness. The censorship obliged him to situate the action in Paris, and the public was astonished to hear Dupont instead of Rodríguez and Mont Blanc instead of the Sierra near Madrid.

The Spanish censorship has been just as hard on illustrations. From 1939 to 1965 not a single nude was published in the Spanish magazines, and when the government printed a stamp with the Maja of Goya they naturally chose the clothed one.

"When he sees beauty every man stumbles."

The primacy of sex in our country has occasioned a scale of values in which the physical aesthetic enjoys a much higher position than it does in other countries. Being pretty helps a woman everywhere, but in Spain it is almost a *sine qua non* for social success, and women who are not pretty go to any length—hairdressers, creams, massage—to appear so.

A beautiful woman is displayed hopefully and proudly. An ugly one is taken out with certain misgivings, and often because there is nothing else to be done. In English, "charming" can refer to an ugly woman; the Spanish equivalent, *encantadora*, cannot. Appearance commands, as in so many other situations. For a man walking with an unattractive woman, the glance of a male friend is always an irrevocable judgment. The poor fellow knows that his friend will be saying to their common acquaintances, "I saw So-and-so with a ghastly girl," and he will have to explain later that it was a distant relation—such ladies may be and at times even should be ugly—whom he could not help accompanying.

For the attractive woman, on the other hand, there are never enough glances. In shops and in banks, in public transport, she is given the best place and the best smile, her problems are solved on the spot. She passes through Spain receiving the affectionate approval of everyone (at the same time, of course, causing the greatest irritation—see Envy).

Curiously enough, the Spaniard does seem to understand when a man is ugly, even though he cannot say when he is handsome. The face is the mirror of the soul, people say, and they often extend this proverb to deny that a man of disagreeable appearance may have any other moral or even intellectual qualities. "How can he know anything with that face he's got?" is an incredible but common Spanish criticism.

> *"From the waist upwards we are all good,*
> *from the waist downwards, rather less so."*

A chaste man is not well regarded in Spain. A man who is known to have no wife or mistress is looked on with a certain suspicion. What's the matter with him? Somebody once revealed to me his doubts as to the virility of a certain man of letters. "Why?" I asked. "Have you found anything odd about him? His way of speaking, his gestures are normal. . . ."

"That's true," the other agreed. "But where's his wife? Or his mistress—eh?"

"But what do we know about it? Mightn't it be that he has one and doesn't want to display her?"

He looked at me in astonishment. What man would have a woman and not display her? No, no, there was something odd. "And religion?" I said. "He might be a very religious man and therefore pure, apart from the flesh."

This idea did not convince him either. Spaniards, however devout they may be, often cannot accept the reality of chastity. There was Lope de Vega, who was not protected from temptation even by his priest's robes. He later repented with the same passion with which he had sinned, wept, agonized, slid back again. "That is our tradition," said my friend, "sin, repent, then start all over again. But it seems to me that your friend . . . eh?"

"Our friend" had become "my friend." He separated himself prudently, just in case. Until such time as the other "proved" his manhood. This was perhaps another example of that same unreasonableness with which Spanish jurisprudence believes an individual guilty until he has been proved innocent, the opposite of the much more humane Anglo-Saxon premise.

Respecting society and its principles, many well-known Spaniards have a "mistress" who shares their public existence—theaters, dances, dinners, cocktails—and whom they leave in her house at night to return to their own and sleep alone. Is this sham necessary? If you want to keep a good reputation in Spain you must sometimes do the opposite of what is done in other countries.

I remember a plumber in Madrid who worked in a hotel. He was a lusty fellow and repairs sometimes supplied him with little adventures. His wife called him to account in connection with this, and the reply he repeated to me was, more or less: "Don't I give you what you need? You know I love you. Are you missing anything? Okay, then. But if a woman makes eyes at me, what do you want me to do? Would you rather have her say your husband was not a man?"

He seems to have convinced her.

The importance of lust in Spanish life is implicitly recognized by Spanish women, who collaborate by making it an obvious part of daily routine. In a country with little female employment, the life of women is largely centered about the need to attract men; in few other parts of the world is more money spent, in proportion to income, on hairdressing and dressmaking.

Our women's certainty that sex is the only thing that could induce a man to leave them, even temporarily, sometimes reaches extremes. Any Spaniard who has been with his mistress for four or five hours and is about to step outside may be questioned and accused:

"Why are you going?"

"I've got something to do."

"I'm sure you're going to see another woman!"

A phrase so flattering to his masculinity that he could not possibly be offended by it.

ANGER

"I go, O Spaniard of lightning and fire,
and leave you victorious.
I leave you pleasant fields
and trembling go from Spain;
for these men, full of anger,
are like lightning without thunder,
which destroys in silence."

—LOPE DE VEGA, *El cerco de Viena por Carlos V*

"The rain is irritating and it is horribly cold. . . . In the room
we enter the eight seats are occupied. . . . We all look at one
another with the characteristic hatred with which we Spaniards
regard each other, and arrange ourselves for sleeping. . . ."

—PÍO BAROJA, *El Globo*, Madrid, January 1, 1903

THE Spaniard, someone once said, is a short man who seems always irritated. We have seen the reason for this appearance in previous chapters. The determination to appear solemn ("Where are you off to looking so serious?" is a usual greeting) goes back to the sixteenth century when a solemn countenance, along with the "fear of God," was the most important thing for a Spaniard. It still is today. A serious appearance which changes to a wrathful one whenever someone offends him is essential. And it is so easy to offend a Spaniard! It is enough to give a fleeting glance to his lady companion, to make a comment aloud which an extreme susceptibility may consider offensive, to brush against his person. A very well known Spanish radio speaker was struck by a man attending a broadcast because he asked the latter's wife the usual question, "señora or señorita?" The wife was in a well-advanced pregnancy and the offended husband thought he saw sarcasm and insult in what had only been absent-mindedness.

The angry aspect of the Spaniard is confirmed by his speech. Besides employing in everyday discourse the tone of voice which other peoples reserve only for bitter disputes, he makes generous use of verbal violence—the interjection. Ortega y Gasset has emphasized this point:

> It is well known that there exist no people in Europe that possess such a rich treasury of insulting words, of oaths and obscenities, as ours; it seems that only the Neapolitans can supply us with any competition.
> . . . We were speaking of indifferent matters. . . . Nevertheless our friend scattered an endless number of obscenities and oaths between his phrases. They were like a beat, like a rhythm which gave a certain architecture to his sentences, as the sharp ashlar stones of the corners and the sharp verticals of the façade do to a building. And our friend obviously felt, each time he let loose an oath, a certain fruition and relief; he felt he needed them as a rhythmic purging of the spiritual

energy which accumulated within him at every moment
and hindered him.

The everyday use of such interjections has not at all weakened the idea that they are bad. The Spaniard therefore has two
vocabularies, one for use with those of his own sex and another
for women. If a man calls out something indecent at a public
show, his friend will take care to remind him, "There are ladies
present, man!" And his conditioning is such that he may go on
calling out as before, but using tamer synonyms beginning with
the same syllable: *Fu*dge, *Ass*tounding, *Bulls*-eyes.

The obscenity is an insult to the world, something abstract
which serves to express the Spaniard's feelings. His anger
makes him seek the most direct way to attack the enemy, and
in his attempt to wound him deeply the most usual method is
to refer to the honor of the man's mother, whom in most cases
he doesn't even know. Obviously, over the years, what was a
clear relation of cause and effect (the son of a woman who
trafficked with her body could not be good) became an arbi-
trary insult. So familiar is the insult, so often repeated the
phrase, that it can be enough simply to say "I was just thinking
of your mother" for all present to know what to expect.

The Spaniard's insistence on this insult makes him wary at
the mere mention of the family, and one must soften one's
voice and gesture when saying, for instance, "Tell that to your
mother." (The thing has not, however, reached the extreme
that it has in Mexico. That country, which in many aspects is
Spain without Europe, that is to say a Spain coarser and tougher
even than the original, has so used and abused the insult to
the mother that it has "burnt up" the name for normal usage.
Nobody can ask a Mexican how his mother is without exposing
himself to verbal violence or a bullet. For such questions, Mexi-
cans resort to *mama*, a diminutive which in Spain is used only
by children, and it is curious to hear a mature man ask a friend
who has a moustache like Pancho Villa's, "How is your
mama?")

And if this is the speech of a civilized Spaniard, how is it

with the more primitive citizen? Antonio Machado did not
spare the adjectives:

> The bad man abounds in the country and the village,
> capable of insane vices and bestial crimes, who under
> his brown smock hides an ugly soul, the slave of the
> seven deadly sins.

The Spaniard's facile anger, combined with his contempt for
others' rights, easily becomes cruelty. Perhaps geography does
not completely explain the behavior of men, but it plays an
important part. The land in Spain has in general a wretched
fertility; it does not foster the inner contentment which in other
lands allows a man to be satisfied with himself and to regard
the defects of others with understanding eyes. Hunger is a bad
counselor, and necessity does not produce feelings which are
exactly humanitarian. Death is seen more as a lottery than as
something horrifying to be forestalled at all costs. Discomfort
makes life itself less desirable, and still less consideration will
be given the life of someone else:

> The mother was praying and said,
> Give us our daily bread. . . .
> The hungry daughter who heard her
> yawned and smiled.

The cruel peasant has been satirized by Gila and Mingote.
The former describes him as capable of bloodthirsty jokes: "We
put a firecracker as big as that in his ear, Jujú! The biggest bit
of him left was like that. . . . His widow got angry and the
festival committee said to her, 'If you can't take a joke, you
can leave the village!' " The inspired cartoonist Mingote always
draws his peasant with a *boina* (a black beret) pulled down to
his eyes, his air a mixture of stupidity and wickedness. Not
many years ago, the boys of a village a few kilometers from
Madrid, after fighting a little cow in the plaza, pulled out its
eye as a joke.

A girl in the province of Toledo was offended when I asked
her whether it was true that they played tiresome jokes on

newlyweds. "Get along with you! It's true that if the bridegroom doesn't treat the lads we tie the two of them on a donkey when they come out of the church and prick the animal so that it goes prancing through the country." Then there is the peculiar humor in this song:

> I married a dwarf—
> to make myself die of laughter.
> I placed the bed high
> and he couldn't get up.

Popular phrases often reflect utter contempt for human sensibility! "Nothing happened to his eye, he carried it in his hand" may serve as an example of the naturalness with which bloody accidents are mentioned in Spain.

If geography has made us familiar with cruelty, history has obliged us to use it in order to survive. Since prehistoric times the Spaniards, situated at a crossroads between Europe and Africa, the Mediterranean and the Atlantic, have seen peoples from other countries arrive to dominate a port or a hill, to teach them to live in this way or that: Phoenicians, Greeks, Carthaginians, Romans, Goths, Byzantines, Arabs, French, Portuguese, English—each of them aggravating a bad situation, playing off one group of Spaniards against another; no clear idea of the whole struggle remains except the tradition of killing, a tradition crowned by the great butchery of the last civil war.

Civil war is no new thing in Spain. Spaniards fought against Spaniards before Spain was constituted as a state (Castile against Aragon, Aragon against Navarre, Leon against Castile), and after (communes of Castile, rising of Catalonia, War of Succession). Political parricide became family parricide. When a Spaniard believes he is right—or, better said, when he is moved by passion and forgets right and wrong—he also forgets the ties of blood. Prince Hermenegild fought against his father, King Leovigild, John II of Aragon against his son Charles of Viana. The brothers Pedro the Cruel and Henry of the Mercedes not only hurled their armies against each other; they fought fiercely, hand to hand, struggling on the ground until

Henry, with Du Guesclin's aid, put an end to his brother and thereby to the obstacle separating him from the throne.

The Spaniard, throughout his history, has had the harsh word, the ready threat. When in other countries they talk of beating, he talks of killing. Iniquities which elsewhere receive moral censure receive in Spain a condemnation to death. A hated politician in other countries is received with shouts of "Down with him!" In Spain that is insufficient. There, the cry is "Let him die," a desire expressed with the same ease as when wishing defeat on a rival soccer team.

Human life generally has little value for the Spaniard. Until a very short time ago—I believe they have reformed it—the judicial penalty for manslaughter was really so slight as to be absurd. In Spanish wars the moment arrives when, to judge by the fiery propaganda, it seems more natural to die for the motherland than to see that her enemies die for theirs; the dead soldier seems to be valued more highly than the conquering soldier.

Contempt for survival is noticeable in all aspects of everyday life. The carelessness with which Spanish workers leave open manholes in the pavement, exposing the passerby to a fall or the motorist to an accident, is an example of the indifference with which the possibility of physical injury is viewed by the people responsible. The newspapers often have to scream about the hole for days and days before the municipality, the state, or the construction company remembers to close it or erect a barrier with a warning light. When such a mistake is corrected it is because the order comes from above, not because it occurs for one moment to the man responsible that the hole represents a danger for anyone who happens by and should be covered even if no one were to order it. If you point out the danger to him he will shrug his shoulders and answer "Let them look out, then."

One day, going from Madrid to Saragossa, I rounded a curve to find myself unexpectedly confronted by a tree in the middle of the road. It had just been cut down by some woodsmen who looked at me in astonishment when I got out of my car to abuse them with insults. They did not understand at all. We were all Spaniards but we were using different languages. I was speaking to them of their immense moral responsibility and they answered that they had a permit from the town hall. "But don't you realize that if you don't put someone with a flag on the curve, anyone may crash into the tree?" No señor, that had not occurred to them. Then they asked me if I had been frightened and offered me a glass of wine. It was the classic Spanish differentiation between the legal and the personal, the abstract and the human. The possibility that the señor, coming along the road without warning, might crash into the obstacle had not penetrated their imagination. But when the señor assumed human shape, they were willing to do everything to help him.

Ortega y Gasset has used strong language in describing the Spaniard's anger: "What a book could be written with the title *Of the Harshness of Spanish Customs.* Just to glimpse what really exists beneath the apparent camaradie of the Spaniards is frightening. In reality a terrible steel spring keeps them separate—ready, if it should give way, to hurl themselves upon each other. Every conversation is about to turn into hand-to-hand combat; every word is a spear thrust; every gesture a slash with a knife. The Spaniard is a center of ferocity which radiates in turn his hatred and contempt." The author was speaking many years before the ordeal by fire of the Civil War.

In a Spanish village, the "lame one," the "stutterer," the "hunchback" are names on everyone's lips; they clearly indicate two things: the deformity or physical defect of an individual, and the cruelty with which his neighbors remind him of it daily. But in censuring these villagers we should remember that people as refined and cultured as the writers of the seventeenth century looked at Juan Ruiz de Alarcón's double hump and called him the "poet between two plates," telling him, "You always were a tortoise and a tortoise you will remain."

This harshness rules as much in the individual as in the group, perhaps more so in the former, since personal offenses for the Spaniard are much more serious than those committed against his community. I have heard persons habitually mod-

erate in judgment raise their voice in a paroxysm of rage over
a trifle: "What should be done to that type is put four bullets
into him!" "People like that don't deserve to live." The disproportion between the sin and the punishment never seems to
strike them.

It will be said that such wishes are only a manner of speaking. But the phrases which are commonly employed, the everyday idioms, indicate the contrary, very much so. They are the
decantation from century to century of a feeling rooted in the
Spaniard. The Civil War demonstrated that between the saying
and the doing there is nothing more than the possibility of carrying it out. Thousands of Spaniards were pulled out of their
houses for their "four bullets," for acts which in other countries
would have earned only a disapproving shake of the head from
their opponents.

To discuss, according to the dictionary, is to express different
ideas. Nothing more. In Spain such an exchange of opinion is
linked in the imagination to fighting. No one is surprised to
hear, "They had a discussion and soon came to blows."

When the Spaniard joins with someone from his village, it is
likely to be for the purpose of attacking members of the
neighboring village. The youthful natives of Entralgo and those
of Lorio, the villages described by Palacio Valdés in *La aldea
perdida*, find it reasonable to visit each others' festivals armed
with cudgels, with which they beat heavily on the heads of their
neighbors. To the writer, a gentleman who in no way loved
violence, this activity seems natural and he describes it without
a word of censure. (Though he worries later on when the
pistols appear—the sticks were all right.) Even the state, which
ought to be a moderating influence, breathes violence. When the
Republic of 1931 created a new police force for the streets, it
did not occur to the powers to call it something like Peace
Police, as in France, or Rapid Police as in Italy. They called it
Assault Police.

The actor Fernán-Gómez was amazed when a Swedish actress
with whom he was working assured him she preferred to see
films in Spain "because the censorship doesn't cut them up

there." There was nothing sarcastic about her remark. She was referring to the scenes of bloody violence, which fall beneath the scissors in Stockholm while passing untouched in Madrid—where the censorship knows that nobody is going to lose sleep over seeing a couple more corpses.

Yes, death is present in many aspects of Spanish life. Spain is one of only two countries in Western Europe (the other is France) that still keep the death penalty. It is also the one which dresses death in colors and converts it into a spectacle: the bullfight. The Foreign Legion slogan was "Long Live Death," and in many places in the South, a wake is a party. Funeral jokes and black humor began in Spain long before they became popular among American students; "I'll hit you with the corpse," says a man, offended by the way in which his relation's body is being treated.

Our cruelty to animals has produced astonishment and horror in foreigners. In Cuenca, an Englishman relates, they throw a cat into a canyon so that its meows as it descends may indicate the depth of the canyon, and the name of the Pass of Despenaperros ("kill dogs," presumably by dropping them over the precipice) is explicit enough to cause the greatest indignation. The Spanish ass, the horse, the mule receive a treatment which horrifies visitors from other countries, especially Anglo-Saxons. It seems as if the Spaniards transfer the violence with which life treats them to those under their care.

Certainly it is true that the Society for the Prevention for Cruelty to Animals tries its best to get the Spaniards into line with other European nations. But its efforts often stumble against the feigned indignation of the authorities when it tries to denounce some outrage—"They do that? That's bad, man," when it is obvious that the sentiment is "Good, and why waste time on such trifles?" In a country where the bullfight is a national fiesta, the SPCA is bound to find a hostile atmosphere, and the most it can attempt is to alleviate the harshness of the customs a little. Thanks to its efforts in the twenties, the picadors' horses were provided with padded breastplates which prevented the spectacle of their entrails lying about on the sand. But then it became obvious that this measure, while lessening the horses' suffering, increased the bulls', as the picador could now sink his lance in with impunity, without thinking about saving the horse from the horns. A similar substitution of victims occurred when Brother Bartolomé de las Casas, ardently defending the Caribbean Indians, managed to stop their working as slaves—by replacing them with Negroes from Africa.

The rage that the Spaniard shows to animals he also shows to plant life, especially to trees. The number of trees felled in Spain appears incredible, particularly over the last few centuries in Castile. Sometimes the reason was war—Moors against Christians, French against Spaniards—when timber provided barricades against the enemy. At other times it was the need to give sheep and cattle more grazing land. But on countless other occasions, tree felling has been motivated by pure and simple hatred of the tree. (We cannot talk of African influence here; the Moslems, as sons of the desert, adore the leaf which guards them from the sun.) In Castile, which has more or less the same climate five months of the year, they cut down the trees out of pure caprice; the forests described in the Poem of the Cid (Robledal de Corpes) and those which surrounded Madrid and made it a hunting center have disappeared; one only believes in their existence when the plough turns up a great stump that was the base of a gigantic species. The Casa de Campo, preserved because it was Crown property, is an oasis of vegetation in a desert.

Do not think this is all a matter of past history. Today the arboricides have a marvelous excuse: the danger of cars' running into the trees. The Spaniards, who have little regard otherwise for public safety, have recently developed a surprising, almost unhealthy conscience about the danger presented by trees. "A tree . . . there's a tree on the curve at kilometer two hundred and twenty-six—cut it down!" Castile, with its hot sun, has seen the disappearance one by one of the trees that gave it shade. The fact that France, with a much milder temperature and a much greater volume of traffic, leaves along both sides of its highways fine beautiful species, is not of the least importance. Those people. . .

Every Spaniard who is hindered by a tree from passing

another car maintains that they must all be cut down, at once! In Madrid, the last few years have seen the disappearance of the great trees of the boulevards, in whose shade thousands of children used to play, as well as those along the Calle de Serrano. There is no reason why they should not also disappear from the Prado, from Recoletos, from the Castellana. Obsessed as ever by the present moment, incapable of looking to the future, the Madrileños do not realize that the problem of transit in the center of the city is not solved by removing a few more trees; this may give them a bit of breathing space, but not a solution. The only possible answer is to close the center of the city to private cars, and that is what they will have to do one day. (Paris and Barcelona have understood this, and there the cars are left parked beneath the trees.)

Is it that the Spaniard (see Envy) is irritated simply because there is something taller than he?

It is quite possible that the Spaniard's innate cruelty is an inheritance from a past time, when killing was not only thought good but was even to be recommended for gaining salvation. I refer to the Crusades, which in medieval Spain animated the idea of slaughter on both sides, Christian and Moslem. If we read the chronicle of a twelfth-century battle superficially we do not know whether it was written by a follower of Christ or Mohammed. They both talk about "wicked infidels" who die, as they should justly die, by an armed hand, while the combatants themselves do not worry too much about falling, since they will go to paradise. In both cases heaven inspires the combatants and hurls them into battle, encouraging them if necessary with a revealed presence. According to Américo Castro, the Spanish Christians invented a saint, Santiago (St. James), as a psychological balance to the cry of "Mohammed" which launched the Moorish Spaniards into combat.

Let us listen to the courtier poet praising the cruelty of the Moorish King Matamid of Seville:

> Hast thou made the lance fruitful with the heads of
>   enemy kings,

because thou sawest that the bough pleases when it is
     in fruit?
and hast thou dyed thy coat of mail with blood of
     their heroes
because thou sawest that beauty adorns itself with red?

"Three hundred lances there were, all with pennants; each killed a Moor with each thrust," the Cid exults. And his men are happy when the blood can run down a raised sword so abundantly that it spreads as far as the elbow.

Ben Al Qutiya describes a horrible ninth-century incident. When the Moslems of Toledo showed signs of rebelling against the Emir of Cordova, the Emir invited the principal men of the city to the fortress for a feast:

> So they did in fact present themselves and were ordered to enter by one door and their horses were ordered to another by which they were to leave. The executioners were placed at the edge of the moat and they cut the throats of all who entered until the number of dead amounted to over 5,300. Much later, it is said, a doctor from Toledo, on approaching the door through which the guests had entered, and finding on his arrival that no one had yet left, said to the Toledans who were around the gate: "My friends, where are those who entered in the morning. I have seen no one who has come back." Then he raised his eyes, saw the vapor from the blood and cried, "O Toledans! I swear to God that the sword is the cause of this vapor, not the smoke from the kitchen."

This happened in A.D. 807. In 1936 an American journalist from the *Chicago Tribune* entered Badajoz a few days after the city had been taken by the Nationalist troops:

> They were young, mostly peasants in blue blouses, mechanics in jumpers. "The Reds." They are still being rounded up. At four o'clock in the morning they are turned out into the ring through the gate by which the initial parade of the bullfight enters. There machine guns await them.
>
> After the first night the blood was supposed to be

palm-deep on the far side of the lane. I don't doubt it.
Eighteen hundred men—there were women, too—were
mowed down there in some twelve hours. There is
more blood than you would think in eighteen hundred
bodies.[1]

In *La forja de un rebelde*, Arturo Barea describes the shoot-
ing of prisoners in the Republican zone:

> The executions had attracted far more people than I
> would have thought possible. Families with their chil-
> dren, excited and still drowsy with sleep, and militiamen
> with their girls were walking along the Paco de la
> Delicias, all in the same direction. Requisitioned cars
> and lorries were passing by. Crowds and cars had col-
> lected at the entrance to the vegetable market and the
> slaughterhouses at the Glorieta. While carts and trucks
> with green vegetables came and went, militia pickets on
> duty meandered around and asked anyone who caught
> their fancy for his papers.
> Behind the slaughterhouses was a long brick wall and
> an avenue with stunted little trees. The sightseers ambled
> from one to the other and made humorous remarks;
> a pitying comment might have provoked suspicion.
> I had expected the bodies. The sight did not shake
> me. There were about twenty of them. They were not
> mangled. I had seen far worse in Morocco and on the
> day before. But I was shaken by the collective brutality
> and cowardice of the spectators.
> Vans which belonged to the City of Madrid arrived
> to collect the corpses. One of the drivers said: "Now
> they're going to water the place and make it nice and
> spruce for tonight." He chuckled. It rang like fear.[1]

In the twentieth century, more than four hundred years after
the separation of Moslems and Christians, soldiers of the two
faiths still sound astonishingly similar. Franco's forces called
the Civil War a Crusade; the Moslems of Egypt or the Yemen

[1] Quoted by Robert Payne (ed.) in *The Civil War in Spain.*

still refer today to any war of theirs as a Holy War against the enemies of their faith.

In the Middle Ages a warrior, Guzmán, was called The Good because he threw his knife to the besiegers of his fortress, who had threatened to kill his son if he did not surrender. In 1936 an army colonel, Moscardó, did practically the same thing when he was notified that his son would die if he did not surrender the Alcázar of Toledo to the Republicans.

The first time I went to Italy I was amazed to see two Romans (one a Fascist and the other a Communist, to judge by their words) arguing for half an hour in the Galeria Colonna without coming to blows. Two Spaniards moved by such different ideas could not disagree nonviolently for more than two minutes. As Ortega y Gasset has pointed out, "Nearly all the words in the political lexicon of our fellow citizens are simple insults. 'Clerical,' on the lips of Liberals, does not mean a man who believes in the utility of the religious orders for the historical well-being of a people; its direct meaning is 'a contemptible man.' 'Liberal' is not the same as a supporter of universal suffrage, but in the mouth of a reactionary comes to mean a shameless man."

The word "meeting" in English means an assembly of persons, sometimes holding different opinions, often to try to solve a problem. *Mitin*, the equivalent word in Spanish, automatically suggests fighting, and such phrases as "There was a meeting" and "They got up a meeting" suggest acts of public violence.

The same idiosyncrasy has made "intolerance," the Spanish word par excellence, so pleasant on the tongue that it has come to be joined with the adjective "holy," producing a phrase which saddened my master and friend Dr. Marañón. "How can intolerance be holy?" he would say. "Intolerance is diabolical."

Sanctified intolerance has seen the disappearance from many Spanish streets and squares of commemorative evidence of formerly illustrious figures. Since the Spaniard never regards things from the long-term point of view, it does not occur to him that the enemy of today may be tomorrow's hero. On the contrary, he tries to put an end to everything that recalls the person, knocking down statues and churches and changing the names of streets. Our neighbors the French do the exact opposite. Paris is full of inscriptions and monuments to people who were fiercely and popularly opposed but remained admired. "Ah, the great King Henry IV . . .," "The delicious Marie Antoinette . . .," "the revolutionary Danton . . .," "the extraordinary Napoleon. . . ." It is not that they have more personalities in their history but that they do not expunge them.[1]

It is the same in the United States where the War Between the States is remembered with ample generosity toward the defeated. General Lee is perhaps more admired and respected than his conqueror Grant, and in novels and films the sympathetic soldiers are often the southerners.

"Before his lady the wooer is braver than Roldán."

Violence is so normal in Spain that anyone who does not feel it pretends that he does, in much the same way as men who, though not especially interested in women, simulate enthusiasm for them in order to keep in with their friends. Many Spaniards use conventional harsh phrases when they are offended, but without real conviction: "I'm going to smash your mouth in," "if I catch you alone," "you'll soon see who my father's son is," and so on. They cannot maintain this attitude very long, and there is naturally a great disproportion between the threat and the deed.

The fake bully has had a long tradition in Spanish literature. The Centurio of *La Celestina*, who offers a list of samples of the evil deeds he can perform without putting them into practice, is a typical example. And Cervantes sang:

[1] The humorous magazine *La Codorniz*, viewing the iconoclastic fury that followed the Civil War, proposed that in order to avoid confusion, only adjectives should be altered, leaving intact the name of the old patrician. For example, the street of the Glorious Pérez could be changed to the street of the Wicked Pérez. Political passion would be satisfied without making it difficult for citizens to find their way.

... I am a man of courage and I say
that what you say, soldier, is true
and whoever says the contrary is a liar.
And then at once
he pulled down his hat, examined his sword,
gave a furtive look, went away—and nothing happened.

There is never a reference in Spanish conversation to an
enemy without a detailed description of what the speaker plans
to do to him when circumstances allow. As it happens, circumstances seldom allow, and as a last resort the offended person
can say he thought it better to drop the matter because "I don't
want to dirty my hands."

*"The dead men you have killed
enjoy good health. . . ."*

The Spaniard's imagination in describing fights can only be
compared with his imagination in relating amorous adventures.
As in the latter case, the battle usually takes place in a distant
place and without witnesses. It normally proceeds like this:
"This guy came in—well, he could hardly get through the
door he was so big. . . . He began to say to me that if this or
that . . . I kept quiet. . . ."
(In both cases, you will note, the protagonist is passive at the
beginning—with the woman because it is elegant to represent
himself as disinterested while she, won over by his masculine
charm, insists; with the bully because the more desperate and
maddened the bully appears, the greater is the contrast to the
speaker's calm.)
"At last he became very tiresome. I warned him: Don't get
yourself into trouble—but he insisted, began to insult me. Oh
boy! I gave him one like this, *pataplán*! Then he begged my
pardon and we had some drinks."
The speaker is normally an insignificant type without any
skill at judo or karate that might justify the strange denouement
of this fight with a man who "could hardly get through the
door," but he insists with an air of absolute sincerity. Of course,

as in the romantic adventures, though it did not happen like that it "must have happened like like" to ensure his good name, his reputation. The real must make way for the fantastic, must adjust itself according to the requirements of reputation.

I once witnessed a fight in the street. After it was over the man who had been attacked explained, "He wanted to punch my face." Someone said, "What do you mean, wanted? He *did* punch you!" "No!" roared the victim, "No one's going to punch *my* face!" There were ten witnesses to the incident, but that did not matter to him; though the blow on his cheek was still smarting, *it had not occurred*. Like Don Quixote, he denied the evidence in the name of the ideal. No one was going to punch *his* face, just as no one was going to pull the Cid's beard. It was demanded by his manhood, by all the history of Spain.

With such phrases as "for me he is finished" and "as if he did not exist," the Spaniard is accustomed to erase a human being from his life, sometimes for all his remaining years. The Spaniard's susceptibility—he is always on guard, always bristling—makes him take as mortal offense what would elsewhere be received with a shrug of the shoulders, and from that moment he "withdraws his greeting" from the offender. It often happens that the latter does not know what it is all about. For the Spaniard can feel equally offended by commission and omission, and taking away someone's job is sometimes less serious than not inviting him to a party. "He didn't remember me when he was giving his dance, so for me he can go to hell."

This possibility of wounding without realization means that people are running into surprises every day. "Why didn't So-and-so say hello to me?" the Spaniard asks himself, diving into his memory to remember what he did. His stupefaction does not generally last long, nor does it end, as would be logical, in his asking his ex-friend the reason for his attitude. On the contrary, his reaction is immediate: "I don't know what's the matter with him, but I don't need him for anything." And now instead of one there are two offended persons who pass each other in the street, who ignore each other so pompously that anyone could see the situation. They pass at a distance of a meter, chins up, eyes fixed on the horizon, as if no human being existed within ten miles.

This attitude, easy on the street, is more difficult when Spanish society obliges, as it often does, the friends of yesterday and enemies of today to attend the same party or gathering. Then you should see the maneuvers they practice in the tiny space, the strategic retreats, the tactical diversions, the evasions, the urgent withdrawal to the bar or to greet someone at the other end of the room, anything to avoid the odious encounter.

The lady of the house naturally knows about most such conflicts in her set, and tries not to invite two enemies at the same time in the same place—because, among other reasons, it might happen that neither of them would come "if that chap's going . . ." (they have by now bereft each other of their names). But as Spanish humors change so frequently, it is not uncommon for the hostess to do a little investigating after fixing date and time: "I say, how do you get on with So-and-so?"—a question which never seems untimely and is answered truthfully. "We're all right (perhaps with an alarmed "Why? has he been running me down to you?"), or "a little cool but we put up with each other," or "I could kill him."

Mutual hatred can proceed from a thousand causes. For example, it can arise from some competitive examination during which things were said that are difficult to forget. In the examinations for Spanish professorial chairs, there is an exercise called the triad, during which the aspirants to the post devote themselves to judging the work of a rival. In principle, only the scientific part of this work should be judged, that is to say the study should confine itself to the work's depth and authenticity, but the Spaniard cannot imagine separating the man from his work, and his natural inclination to personalize the abstract leads him to attack his competitor not only in his writings but in his person. I attended one session in which one of the competitors denied that another had been in the archives of modern history at Simancas and to prove this produced a paper signed by the secretary of these archives stating he had not seen him there. The other counterattacked with a receipt from a shop in

Simancas where he had bought some pencils—and in his turn threatened to bring to light certain little political secrets. . . .

Many Spanish enmities have been born of the "injustice" committed against the loser of a competitive examination. (While the triad system seems completely absurd, I sometimes think that it shows a certain cleverness on the part of the Spanish state, which by arranging for citizens to quarrel among themselves splits them apart and thus compromises any united front they might muster against higher authority.) I need not add that many of these injustices are real and have been committed for political reasons, which in the postwar period had such influence on Spanish affairs that even in the case of a just appointment people would talk of favoritism because that was all they were accustomed to seeing. The persecution of members of organizations charged with being subversive was taken advantage of by those who wanted to occupy their posts in the state administration.

In the villages, quarrels are kept up for generations, and the inescapable contact imposed by village confinement makes the frown sterner, the gesture harsher. Everywhere in Spain there are Capulets and Montagues, sometimes not even remembering how their resentment began. At times the quarrel is kept alive at the cost of considerable money. Lawsuits are initiated for some wretched cause (a fruit tree against a wall, a right of way) and are kept going year after year without any hope of economic restitution (the lawsuit soon costs more than it could win), only because of the anger provoked by the very idea of abandoning the fight and letting the neighbor think he is right.

Even though the Spaniard's sound may be greater than his fury, cruelty is abundantly present in his mental constitution. Don Juan is famous as a deceiver of women; it is curious that no one refers to him as a killer of men. Nevertheless, the famous wager was two-edged: "Dead men in duels and women made fools of." The dead men comprise a smaller list than the women, but there is no significant reason why it should not be the other way around. After all, Don Juan needed several days for deceiving a woman ("One for winning their hearts, another for bedding them, one for replacing them and one hour for forgetting them"), while for taking a man's life, just the few minutes of a duel were enough.

When Goya, that most Spanish of painters, depicted scenes of popular life, he painted with blood. I am not speaking now of the *Disasters of War*, which after all reflects an exceptional moment in the life of the Spanish people, the War of Independence, but of that remarkable picture in which two peasants are attacking each other with cudgels. If the subject of the painting were a normal fight, the only comment about it could be how artistic the episode is, how worthy of being put on canvas. What makes this fight exceptional is that the two peasants have buried their legs up to their knees, to make the flight of the coward or the weaker one impossible.

Anyone who has talked to a Spanish peasant will have noticed the harshness of his verbal expressions. "Well I never! One of your eyes has popped out!" a gamekeeper at Aranjuez said in my presence to another whose eye was only bloodshot. If you give police authority to a village Spaniard, you put into his hands, along with the gun, an outlet for his wrathful instincts. There was a park keeper I knew in the Casa de Campo for whom any offense within his jurisdiction, beginning with the stealing of a little firewood, deserved the sternest punishment. "If I catch him I'll have to give him a couple of bullets, to put an end to that breed! Don't you think so?" He looked at me, his eyes full of rage which promptly turned to astonishment when I said no, I believed that a man's life was worth more than four twigs from a tree.

"There's no worse wedge than one that is made from the same wood," says a Spanish proverb, or, "When they make a base man lord, there's no more cruel despot."

These sentiments are realized in many situations. Spanish pride is much more important than class ties, and the official harshest to workmen or peasants is invariably a man who rose from their ranks.

Cruelty is sometimes admired romantically. Some years ago in Madrid there was the famous case of a certain Jarabo who killed three persons in order to rob them. The crime, hateful from every point of view, had special circumstances which surprisingly led many people, especially women, to side with the murderer. He was handsome, of good family, and had been rich until his mad ways dissipated his fortune. He was a Don Juan, and the comment "What a guy! how awful!" often had a tinge of admiration, more obvious on the part of the lower-class women but manifest in most female Madrileños.

For years killing was an open spectacle. When my father was a child, executions were still public, and the custom was to take young boys to them and, when the head of the condemned man slumped on his chest, to give them a clout so that the memory would stay fixed in their minds.

"Here lies half of Spain: killed by the other half" said Larra in his *El día de difuntos de 1836.*

The Spaniard's love for bloodthirsty, macabre pictures and statues has often been studied. The figures of the Holy Week floats have their wounds reproduced with the greatest realism; the thorns really seem to be sticking into the Lord's flesh, the swords into the heart of the Virgin of the Sorrows. Baroque art showed martyrs beheaded, flayed, nailed to a cross; it tried to produce both physical shock and compassion for the innocent who suffered for the true religion. If the sculptor did not succeed in winning the admiration of the public for the artistic perfection of his work, at least he could obtain a violent shudder for the overflowing wounds (more red paint) which the Lord received in his passion.

The same kind of motive, seeking to stir physical and moral sensibilities at the same time, is found in the secular art of Valdés Leal, where the corpses of bishops and kings are shown in their aristocratic decay, with the worms preying among silks, scepters and crosiers.

This painter's two most famous canvases are kept in a building in Seville whose name is for me an example of a much greater cruelty than the pictures and statues I have mentioned. The building is known as the Hospital of the Incurables. For centuries it has seemed natural to the Spaniard of Seville to use this name for an institution to which one day, in the normal course of things, he may have to take one of his family.

"Come on father . . . , we're taking you to the hospital, you'll be well looked after there. . . ."

"To which hospital, my son?"

"To the Incurables."

Cruelty is probably the Spanish characteristic most widely known abroad. The diagnosis is correct but the symptoms are usually mistaken, being based on half-truths. Spaniards are cruel, but not *that* cruel.

When it is said, for example, that the Spanish Inquisition tortured its victims, something is stated which although true has no value as an example unless we add that in that age *all* religious and secular courts tortured their prisoners as a legal means of making them confess. In this perspective, the behavior of the Inquisition can be seen with less disgust, even if the belief persists that the Holy Office, because of its religious nature, ought not to have resorted to such harsh procedure. (The bad thing about the Inquisition, as Dr. Marañón saw very well, was not the physical brutality but the spiritual, not the man who would torture bodies but rather the man who would try to torture souls, who would persecute ideas and attempt to eradicate those he did not like from the most sacred and inviolable parts of a man's conscience.)

While they tortured in Spain they did so also throughout Europe, and in the Dutch museums, beside the instruments of torture for the Protestants, are those used against the Catholic priests. Mary Tudor was called "Bloody" because the blood she shed was Protestant; the victory of that faith in England decided the nickname. If things had turned out differently, Mary might have been "the Arm of the Faith," or something like that.

Unluckily for the Spaniard, his chief enemies in the sixteenth and seventeenth centuries were also the best printers of the time. The world, just beginning to read, was inundated with pamphlets—for the illiterate there were engravings—which showed Spanish cruelty to Protestants and American Indians.

Spanish cruelty in America was in fact restrained by covetousness—no one puts an end to the instruments of work—and by lust. The Spaniard did not discriminate against women of other races as did—in public at least—the Anglo-Saxon and the Dutchman, but actually filled the southern continent with half-castes who ended up throwing him out. What is certain is that the characteristic features of the Indian remain prevalent in millions from Mexico to Cape Horn, while in what is today the United States and Canada you have to look, with map in hand, for the "reservations" where they guard the nearly extinct species of the Redskin. It will be admitted that as race murderers the Spaniards were pretty inefficient.

The Spaniard did not want to destroy any people even though he tried to impose his authority on all. There was no "genocide" during his history and the oppressed could always choose to leave (Jews, Moriscos).

The Spaniard's cruelty is a vital circumstance of the harshness which has surrounded him since childhood. There is no sadism in him; he accepts pain, blood, and death as an integral part of human life, but he does not enjoy contemplating them, nor does he like to see them exaggerated.

Let us look at the most obvious case, the bullfight. Anyone, moved by a desire to exchange the black legend for an equally unrealistic white one, who maintains that there is no cruelty in this spectacle, ought to be admired more for his patriotism than for his logic. A fiesta at which six bulls are attacked with lances and darts and killed with a sword, and where the two other participants (the horse and the man) risk a mortal wound, cannot help but be cruel (nor does the fact that other equally cruel spectacles exist elsewhere lessen the cruelty).

But the cruelty to the bulls is conditioned by and subjected to the development of the fiesta. I know no good fan who "likes" the picador episode. When the pic sinks into the bull's hump there are signs of attention—"It's well (or badly) placed,"—but I have never seen anyone lick his lips with pleasure at the jet of blood staining the animal's side. And so precise is the relationship between the pic and its function of lowering the bull's head that the slightest indication that the picador has sunk it in deeper than is necessary produces the most violent protests. If the public errs in its judgment it is always against the picador. They scream at him, often unjustly. This abuse of a man who is simply doing his job is an example of the antipathy with which the public in general views his sanguinary action.

The same thing happens when the matador takes a long time killing the bull, when the sword enters uselessly or the *descabello* fails time after time. If the bullfight public were really cruel, if it really, as some foreigners like to believe, went to the ring "to see the bull suffer," it would applaud this prolongation of the agony. Those who are in the ring—especially the matador who hears whistling and insults and sees the possibility of the award of an ear which his previous performance has deserved slipping away from him—know only too well that true cruelty is not their motive.

The man kills the wild animal in front of a large public. Maybe this is cruel. But he must kill it from straight in front with his right hand, putting his arm between the bull's horns. That is justice. The bull must die because the laws of the bullfight have been made by men and not by bulls, but he must die without having his horns shaved, without the matador's having an excessive advantage because the bull is lame or poorly endowed with horns. (All matadors, the most skillful as well as the most clumsy, bear on their bodies scars which reveal the bull's capacity for defense, without which there is no bullfight).

Sadism is a mental attitude toward pain, an intellectual delight in another's suffering. Spanish cruelty, on the contrary, is direct, on the surface, I would even say "healthy." The proof is that there has never been in Spain the type of literature catering to masochistic or sadistic readers, a genre to which Anglo-Saxons are given. Spanish cruelty (like lust) is not repressed or stifled, and thus does not need to find expression in fiction.

The Spaniard is not cruel on an immediate, everyday basis.

A beggar in Spain has every possibility of earning a living by his begging. The Spaniard will do nothing to prevent it. It is true that organizing committees to help those whom fortune has disinherited would require a capacity for collective action which the Spaniard does not possess, but show any citizen of the peninsula or its islands an unfortunate man and he is likely to go to his assistance, however poor he may himself be.

Some years ago there was in Madrid a little boy who went about with a tray of cakes. He would suddenly pretend to stumble and the cakes would fall to the ground. The boy would begin to pick them up between sobs, while the passersby gathered around him. He would explain, weeping, that his master would make him pay for the cakes he had spoiled, and in a few minutes would have a large number of pesetas in his hands. The boy would thank the people, pick up his cakes and go off to another corner of the city to repeat the same game. It was only after several weeks of such "accidents" that the police stepped in and the business ended; up to then it had not failed a single time.

GLUTTONY

"The Spaniards . . . sparing in eating and sober in drinking but superfluous in dressing."

—BALTASAR GRACIÁN, *El Criticón*

"The first commandment of the poor:
burst rather than leave anything on the table."

GLUTTONY

EATING

THE current estimate of the Spaniard agrees with Gracián's thesis. Others have pointed out that the Spaniard is sober for the simple reason that he cannot be anything else. It is obvious that most of his domain is hardly a paradise of temptations; the brown plateaus, the harsh mountains suggest nothing to the appetite. The people of these regions eat very little. There is a famous anecdote of Eugenio d'Ors in which he describes the sensation of sadness afforded him by a Castilian village with only one square, in the square only one shop, and in its window only one tortilla, with a card saying "Sold."

The tendency of history and language to associate Spain with Castile has maintained this antigluttony concept of the Spaniard for years. The most famous writers echo it. For the one time that Sancho Panza eats well (Camacho's wedding, at the house of the Gentleman with the Green Coat) he goes hungry a hundred others. Hunger is described in all picaresque novels with such precision and acuteness as to make us think that the author, whatever his social position, has himself had occasion to know it. (Note the Hidalgo in *Lazarillo*, the beginning of the Buscón in Dómine Cabra's house, and so on.) The Spain which dominated almost the entire world was incapable of feeding her children regularly.

Even so, according to many seventeenth-century writers, what Spaniards had was already too much. Quevedo complains of the softness which has entered Spanish life and goes on to say that Spain's decadence began with the arrival of spice, that refinement of the table:

> The wrinkled peppercorn had not come
> to flatter the taste,
> nor the fragrant exotic adulation
> of the clove.
>
> Mutton and beef were the beginning and the end;
> and with red peppers and tough garlic
> the slave ate as well as the lord.

155

Old-fashioned diners stuck to what they called jack, queen, and king, the three courses. Spaniards of the twentieth century are distinguished from other Europeans by two things: what they eat and when they eat. Today, despite the post-civil-war scarcity of luxuries and the emphasis on weight control, Spaniards continue to eat much more than the majority of the inhabitants of the globe, including the famous Germans and Dutch. The Spaniard has a light breakfast, a few snacks in the morning, a large midday meal (the *cocido* with all its additions is considered only one dish), more snacks, and at least two main dishes at dinner. The "snacks" he has in the bar before going home would suffice for the luncheon of those richest people in the world, the Americans.

I am sure this comparison will cause surprise in my country. The Spaniard considers himself to be poor and therefore believes that in any other country with more resources the food must be richer and more plentiful. Moreover, the Spaniard who boasts about so many things is extremely modest when referring to what he consumes. I have taken part in the following dialogue an infinite number of times:

"I hardly eat a thing. . . ."

"But I've seen what you've ordered. Soup—"

"—A few mouthfuls . . ."

"Fish—"

"—Two tiny mullet, tiny ones . . ."

"Meat—"

"—A little fillet I could hardly see . . ."

"Salad—"

"—That doesn't count. . . ."

"Cheese?"

"Must have something for after . . ."

When I return to Spain from my trips abroad and go to eat with friends I always cause amazement. "Are you ill?" is the affectionate question when I order only a chop cooked in bread crumbs with vegetables, a salad and fruit. "Are you ill? What's the matter with you?"

The proof of how much the Spaniard eats is the price he pays to digest it. In all restaurants and bars it is a normal thing for bicarbonate of soda to be provided free for customers who want it. This is not the case in any other country in the world, so far as I know. When the Spaniard feels "heavy" after eating he hardly ever attributes it to having consumed too much. What happened was that something "didn't agree with me."

Within these generalities we must remember that the geography of gluttony in Spain is as varied as the country's topography. Broadly speaking, the cult of the meal descends from north to south and from east to west.

The greatest food lovers are the Basques, while the Andalusians are the poorest; the succulent food of the Levante is transformed into simple dishes in Salamanca and Extremadura. (A meal's being heavy does not make it a case of Gluttony with a capital letter. Dishes based on pork are generally heavy, and the only thing this usually indicates is that pork is cheap in the region.)

At the top of Spanish cuisine we clearly find Basque cooking. At the top of Spanish eating we clearly find the Basques. Nobody denies them this primacy, which starts with the raw materials: meat from lands high in humidity, fish—perhaps the best in the world—from Cantabrian streams. These are prepared with minute attention to detail, and at last comes the almost religious ecstacy with which the diners sit down to table. The jokes of the Basques generally feature one of two subjects: the Basque's distrustfulness, or his gigantic appetite. Probably the best-known one is about the Bilbao man who was presented with a series of gastronomic possibilities and asked what he was capable of devouring. The Basque replied that he could manage a small calf, a couple of lambs, three dozen fowls . . .

"And sparrows?"

"Sparrows?" The man looked around him in astonishment. "Sparrows?—Every one of them!"

Less notorious are the Catalans, family men who do not much like going out to dine but who also are hearty eaters. Their special dishes of green and white beans on rice are only a prologue to fish and chops with an accompaniment of potatoes and greens.

The Asturians are not far behind with their basic dish, based on haricot beans and pork, the famous *fabada*. Asturias was the land of Palacio Valdés, who in the *Alegría del Capitán Ribot* provided one of the few examples in Spanish literature of sensuality in the description of a meal.

To find the other best writings on food we must turn to two men from Galicia, a province which competes with the Basque country in the produce of its land and sea, but whose natives, perhaps for economic reasons, do not consume the same quantities of food as the men from Vizcaya and Guipúzcoa. (Alava, more Castilian, is also more temperate.) These two Galicians are Julio Camba and Wenceslao Fernández Flórez.

To Julio Camba we owe the most famous book on Spanish cuisine of modern times, *La casa de Lúculo*. Teaching by example, Camba was completely intolerant on the subject of food and, as many of his friends knew by experience, refused invitations unless he could choose the restaurant, the food, and the wine. Fernández Flórez was no less convinced of the importance of food. He wrote many articles against the custom of banquets, for he affirmed that "There is no friendship which makes it worthwhile to eat stale crayfish,"[1] and when his fellow Galicians of Madrid offered him a banquet he refused. "What would people say if, after I have held to my theory for so many years, I changed it because they offered a banquet to me?" he said. "I can't go." "That Fernández Flórez is always joking," thought the organizers. "Don't forget, next Saturday . . ." The banquet was held without the man whom it was intended to honor. His empty chair was kept at the table as a symbol, and the

---

[1] With regard to banquets, he was absolutely right. The violent arguments which occur at them (see Envy) may be partly due to the irritation caused by the food. There appears to be no restaurant, however good it may be, capable of serving a worthy meal to more than twenty persons. And the disappointment is unfortunately irrevocable. Eugenio d'Ors noted, "A bad dinner is something one can never make up for." It is curious that we risk it continually. There are few other countries where banquets are given with such prodigality and for such varied reasons. Once in Madrid we gave a dinner for a writer who was known to be unlucky and a failure, and only for this reason. I do not know if we were moved by charity or satisfaction.

speeches were directed to it. Later they took the flowers from
the center of the table to his mother.

Fernández Flórez was the opposite of Camba; he was courtesy personified and his efforts to avoid wounding his host
while at the same time saving his delicate and demanding palate
were amusing. When he was offered a gin—this happened in
my house—his aquiline profile sharpened in an expression of
mixed joy and distrust, hoping that the name of the gin would
be announced. When he heard it was Gordon's his face lit up
and he accepted delightedly.

In his novels, he treated more keenly than any other writer
the triumphs and sorrows of the glutton, the triumph of devouring and the sorrow at seeing the meal finished, the triumph of
chewing something from his own plate and the sorrow of seeing
something he also wants to eat disappearing from his neighbor's
plate. The banquet of "the fat cows" in *Las siete columnas*
provides a perfect description of the glutton and his philosophy:
"Fatness is peace. . . . No fat man can take part in a war,
because he cannot stand it physically. . . . To feed the peoples
is to procure complete happiness."

All the great eaters I have known did all they could to avoid
crossing the eating frontier, a line running a little below the
suckling pig of Segovia and the partridges of Toledo. For the
gourmet, that is where the great culinary desert begins—
Andalusia.

It is obvious that Andalusians do not eat, though they continually pretend to. There is no one in the whole of Spain who
sits down with less pleasure to a table heaped with food. Yet
there is no one in Spain who more enjoys standing hours and
hours at a bar heaped with snacks. It is not true that the
Flamenco does not eat. The Flamenco eats, but standing up in
order to service the glasses of wine which keep slipping down
his throat. The variety of Spanish snacks, especially Andalusian ones, is incredible, and the sum of those squids, hard
boiled eggs, octopuses, sardines, tiny dishes of this and that,
would constitute a normal meal in many European and American countries. But in Andalusia they do not call it a meal, and

when they try to cook one in the northern style it is an unbelievable imitation. The skill of the Andalusian cook is seen in fried fish, "recently pulled from the bottom of the sea," as Juan Carlos de Luna says in the *Piyayo*, and in the creation of a dish which, like *paella*, has crossed all the frontiers of the world. I refer to *gazpacho*, whose inventor hundreds of years ago unwittingly discovered in this fruit and vegetable dish a source of remarkable nutritional value. He also discovered that with the temperature 100° F. in the shade, the olive gatherer or the vine pruner cannot eat a meal that is hot and heavy, and that he needs something which serves as both food and drink. Thus was born this dish which is both liquid and solidly nourishing.

Apart from *gazpacho*, which is a regional dish, although when summer arrives it becomes a national and even a universal one, the dishes which appear most often on Spanish tables are *cocido* and *paella*. The reason for their success is that their basic ingredients, rice, potatoes, chick-peas, are found easily and cheaply all over the peninsula. And with the regional barrier thus easily crossed, the socio-economic one is also overcome without effort—these elastic dishes may cost much or little, depending on the kind and number of "bits and pieces" that are included in them.

DRINKING

Wine is produced over much the greater part of the Spanish countryside, often more plentifully than water—witness the custom of the Monegros of exchanging a liter of wine for one of water, or the Andalusian houses built with wine in the mortar. From the Galician Riveiro to the wine of Panades, from the wines of La Rioja to those of Jerez de la Frontera, through the Valdepeñas region of central Spain which produces the cheapest and therefore most common Spanish wines, an ocean of fermented grape juice spreads over the country like a stain, and after passing down Spanish throats in impressive quantities still allows large exports and fame abroad, such as sherry (Jerez) has enjoyed since the times when Shakespeare praised it.

The Andalusian Spaniards who followed Mohammed sometimes forgot his antialcoholic advice, as this twelfth-century
poem makes clear:

> The light of dawn surprised us with our cheeks resting
> on the palms of our hands.
> All night I had not stopped pouring them wine, nor
> myself drinking what remained in their glasses until I
> became as drunk as they.
> But the wine took a good revenge. I had made it fall
> down my throat and it made me fall on the ground.

Fortunately this kind of disequilibrium is not common in
Spain. In some contradiction to the map we have marked out
for eating, the greatest consumption of wine is in the North
and South, the Basque provinces and Andalusia. Basques and
Andalusians, so different in all other aspects of their lives, share
the practice of singing after prolonged libations. This singing
may be choral in a Bilbao tavern or solo in a Seville street, as
choral and solo as the respective dances of the same regions,
but the effect is the same. A man feels obliged to hurl through
his throat the happiness with which he is overflowing and to let
the heavens share it.

What is misleading about the Spaniard's drinking habits is
that excesses usually occur on occasions when the country is
full of foreigners. If a tourist travels in Spain only during the
fiesta of San Fermín in Pamplona or Holy Week in Seville, for
the rest of his life no one will convince him that the Spaniard
is not a hopeless drunkard, in whatever latitude he lives.

Of course this is not true. On the contrary, the average Spaniard is unbelievably sober, particularly if we take into account
the fact that the price of wine is within the reach of any workman and even any beggar. With the tavern a temptation on
every corner, where the company of friends stimulates the great
Spanish vice of conversation, with football games and bullfights
to discuss, the Spaniard is, I repeat, unbelievably sober. Perhaps
it is because he has been drinking from childhood, at least while
he eats: "A meal without wine is a stingy meal." And just as
the famous king of antiquity protected himself against poison

by taking tiny amounts of it, thus accustoming his body to the reaction, the Spaniard has been immunized against the surprises of drink. But probably the basic reason lies elsewhere. A drunk man makes a fool of himself, and this is the danger the Spaniard fears most (see Pride). Hence when we meet a drunk man he tries to convince us that he is not drunk, insisting that he's "not being objectionable to anybody," an absurd defense which only points up what *is* objectionable, the fact that he is not behaving like a gentleman. When the Spaniard gets drunk, he contrives, like the Englishman, that it shall not be noticed; but whereas the Englishman, in accordance with his character, becomes more reticent, remaining motionless in his corner so that no movement shall betray his downfall, the Spaniard, more extroverted, goes around trying to convince each person present that he is not drunk and that he is a gentleman.

Spanish ethics and morals—in line with those of other countries—have been greatly relaxed in the last few years, but the wonderful stigma of drunkenness still persists. "Drunk" is still an insult; "He takes wine badly" is still a warning to avoid a person. Anglo-Saxon society, so severe in many aspects of life, tolerates, accepts, and forgives the guest who gets drunk at a party. It seems to the Anglo-Saxon to be something natural in a man's life. Spanish society, much laxer about other sins—especially, as we have seen, lust—flatly refuses to tolerate the spectacle of a man deprived of his senses, and a guest in this state can be sure that he will not be invited again. (Of the innumerable parties of my life I remember only one instance when a guest made such a first and last mistake.) Judgment is usually severe and final: "If he doesn't know how to drink he'd better not drink." When the Spaniard, aware of the public attitude, has unwittingly reached this condition, he resorts to his best dialectic. It is never that he has drunk too much, but that he has mixed his drinks—and we all know that is bad.

The idea of a drunk man does strike the Spaniard as funny in principle, and jokes multiply about the type who doesn't know what he wants apart from the obvious necessity to go on drinking. Spaniards do not drink much water—"There must be something bad about water if they have to bless it," goes a saying—and in general they talk of wine as if they could not live without it, which again contributes to the mistaken idea that some foreigners form of Spanish drinking.

Different nationalities treat the question of drink in different ways. The Nordic man, in general, sees drink as a way of escape from a reality which torments him. This reality may be the climate in Scandinavia, the pressure of work in the United States, or some professional or personal problem. The mission of the liquor, therefore, is precisely to "knock him out" of that reality and transport him to another world, exactly as in the case of drugs. It is not by chance that in the countries where people drink a lot there are also many cases of suicide. It is not that they kill themselves because alcoholism leads them to it. It is that death is the only exit left open to them when drink is no longer enough to free them from their problems.

In Spain, on the contrary, they do not drink to get away from society but to make it more pleasant. The Spaniard who drinks feels more communicative, more self-confident—if that is possible—and ready to explain to this society what he thinks about the problems of life. Alcohol suggests new ideas to him, supplies him with excitement and, at the same time, new avenues to explore. As he drinks he sees himself taller, handsomer, more intelligent, especially more brilliant. For this reason, at the first stutter, at the first mistake, the Spaniard checks himself. His desire is to triumph in this society, not to be exiled from it and vanish into the night.

And besides, he must maintain his dignity. I remember a friend of mine at a party, many years ago. His drinking had put him dangerously near unconsciousness and he was making pretty speeches to an adolescent girl, a sister of the hostess. His wife went up to him and I only heard these words: "You're making a fool of yourself." That was enough.

ENVY

~~~~~~

"No man is a prophet in his own country. This is particularly true in Spain. Its inhabitants envy the learned man who rises among them and attains mastery in his art; they think little of the great things he may do, belittle his successes and gloat, on the other hand, when he falls or stumbles, above all while he is still alive, with twice the animosity of any other people. . . . If fortune later leads him along the road where he clearly excels his rivals . . . then war is declared on the unfortunate man, who becomes nourishment for murmurings, fodder for slanders, a magnet for censures, the prey of tongues, and the target for attacks on his honor."

—*"Risala apologetica de Ibn Mazam,"* eleventh century, trans. and ed. García Gómez

"To see you blind, the envious man would pull out one of his own eyes."

THE fact that the most generous people in the world are probably also the most envious is one of the many paradoxes of the Spanish makeup. If there is one thing that annoys the Spaniard it is that another should distinguish himself, should rise in the world. Antonio Machado sang:

> The ever-troubled eye of envy or of sadness
> guards its prey, bewails its neighbor's achievements.
> Its ill luck does not pass, it does not enjoy its wealth;
> both fortune and misfortune wound and grieve it.

Like the glutton who while eating never takes his eyes from his neighbor's plate, the envious man cannot be content if another possesses something that he fancies. That is why one of the most difficult things for the Spaniard to do is to praise another.

It is so difficult that the language contains various formulas for softening praise, however well deserved it may be. One example is an expression which is so natural and often repeated today that those using it probably do not realize its meaning as the symbol of an attitude: "We must admit that So-and-so is a good actor (or engineer or tie salesman)." That is, we must make an effort, we must oblige ourselves much against our wishes to grant virtue to the person in question. I have never heard anyone say, "We must admit that So-and-so has a defect." For this, no softening is needed. One need not torment himself to find an adjective for running someone down. Perhaps this attitude lies behind the Spanish habit of saying, "That's an ugly girl" when the prettiest girl in town passes, or "Her father left her barefoot" when she has millions. The speaker's intention is clear without his having to use the hated compliment.

Let us suppose that a man has been granted success, has cleared this first barrier, and that, swallowing hard, another recognizes his worth in some field. Then will come the qualification: "Yes, but as a person," or, if the man is a good person, "But as an engineer." The praise will never be absolute, it will always carry a qualification behind it like a tail. The Spaniard urgently has to find something about the admired person which will muddy his admiration and lessen some of its weight. How often have we heard, "How clever the bastard is" or, even more seriously and with an affectionate smile, "How well the son of a bitch writes." This, even if it does not look like it, is praise, the greatest praise a Spaniard can offer. The coarse word has no real meaning; it is necessitated by the compliment, like a customs duty which the person praised has to pay.

The thing about Spanish envy is that it takes very little, hardly anything, to arouse it. Jardiel Poncela, who was short, was irritated by Americans because of their height. This magnificent writer considered the very fact of their existence a continual offense. "There's no need to be so tall," he would murmur indignantly when some six-footer passed near him. I have heard many friends who in other respects show generosity and nobility say in irritation, "Look at the way that chap shows off." When I ask, "What is he showing off about?" the answer is incredible: "Can't you see? About women, about being good-looking!" "But have you spoken to him?" "That's not necessary. You only have to see how he enters places *avasallando*" (that is, automatically converting those present into his vassals). I looked and could only see a good-looking young man who had come into the café with an attractive blond. I never saw him look contemptuously at anyone or display the lady with a mocking air as if to say, "Here she is, I bet you haven't anything like her, have you?" I wonder what he might have done to earn forgiveness. Come in again, wearing a torn and dirty shirt, accompanied by a plain girl?

The Spaniard can tolerate one or two admirable qualities in another Spaniard but never more. A man may be rich and a nobleman, but not also intelligent, clever or witty. As soon as he tries for a third distinction, animosity is unleashed. "Who the hell do you think you are, man?"

"Talent and money are not good companions."

I remember one reply of the many that Augustín de Foxá made famous. Aristocratic, rich, a diplomat, he had just married a very pretty girl; he was the favorite guest in the houses of Madrid, and as if that were not enough, his verse play *Baile en Capitanía* was filling the theater. When I congratulated him in the vestibule of the Teatro Español he said, "It's a lot, isn't it? I've started a rumor going that I have a stomach ulcer."

He knew his world. At any gathering, after the required "We must recognize . . ." someone would say, "Yes, what a shame he's so ill," and everyone in their hearts could feel relieved. We can't tolerate some people having everything and others nothing, *caramba*!

When after the Civil War Ortega y Gasset gave a series of lectures in Madrid, I heard more than one person criticize the *audience*. The presence of many elegant ladies in the hall exasperated a number of intellectuals who, being poor, refused to admit that a person rich in goods could be so in brains as well, probably because this would make *them* seem still poorer.

When a literary or artistic work has reached such heights of fame that it is impossible to despise it without seeming absurd, or when we like it "in spite of ourselves," it may always be compared with other works by the same author. The country which invented the saying "All comparisons are odious" did so because it could not conceive of two objects deserving equal praise.

And so we hear, "Yes, the work's not bad, but it's the only one he's produced that's any good."

And if, made vain by success, the author attempts a sequel, he will hear that "second volumes are never good," a saying obviously created to preserve the tranquility of the envious. "The second one can't be as good, I tell you!"

And this is said and popularly believed in the nation which saw the publication of the two parts of *Quixote*!

The almost physiological need to reproach men at the top reduces the Spanish critic to the meanest and most ludicrous attacks. The enemies of Pérez Galdós, for instance, referred to him in the newspapers simply as "Señor Pérez," with which they evidently thought to make the novels, *Episodios nacionales*, and plays of this genius disappear through a trap door.

When I read in the preface to a new book, "At the affectionate request of my friends I have collected my writings from here and there," I cannot avoid a certain skepticism. I do not believe there are many Spaniards who urge a compatriot to publish something unless they are quite sure it will be a failure.

And when the saying "It's only one step from the sublime to the ridiculous" is applied to a man, I always have the impression that the speaker is trying to shove him into taking it.

When faced with two outstanding reputations—in any field, whether literature, theater, or sport—the Spaniard's admiration for one must be accompanied by hatred for the other. In Pérez de Ayala's time, Spanish glories seemed to come in pairs— Calvo and Vico, actors; Cánovas and Sagasta, politicians; Castelar and Salmerón, orators: Galdós and Pereda, novelists— and the bitterness he describes in his account of the various rivalries would be just as valid in modern Spain:

> Citing the names together implied irreducible opposition, equivalent to the first and the last, alpha and omega, good and evil, Ormuz and Ariman, God and the Devil. The fan of the torero Lagartijo preferred and praised any other bullfighter rather than Frascuelo; the Frascuelo enthusiast applauded mediocre bullfighters but never found anything good about the fighting of Lagartijo. The journalist who ranked all writers after Pereda put Galdós at the end; for the Galdonianos it was vice versa. In Congress, Canovistas came to blows with Sagastianos, Salmeronianos with Castelarinos. In the theater Vico's fans fought with Calvo's, Gayarre's with Masini's.

The Spaniard can also counteract praise by censuring a relative. If a person is being talked of with admiration there will be someone who says after a short pause, "The son hasn't turned out the same, has he? No such luck," or, "The brother is worth nothing compared to him—naturally!" Thus the great poet Manuel Machado ended up as "the bad Machado" because he was brother to the immense Antonio. In the case of the Alvarez Quintero brothers, whose identity as a team stubbornly resisted individual comparisons, a legend was created. Neither of the

two was the good one. The "good one" was a hunchbacked
brother whom they allowed no one to see, and it was he who
dictated the plays which Serafín and Joaquín afterward signed.
(This was the version I heard many years ago. I discovered
later that a sick brother had in fact existed, but nobody ever
came up with any proof of his literary paternity. It was simply
easier to believe that a deformed man might write interesting
things which earned money. Poor fellow, he had to amuse himself with something!)

Considering this spirit, which has given rise to the incredible
proverb "Think the worst and you'll be right," it is not strange
that slander should flourish in Spain, a country used to bringing
personalities down to a level which allows them to be accepted
by ordinary citizens. Since the earliest Spanish society—the
Spanish poet Martial was distinguished during the Roman
Empire for his biting tongue—our habit has always been to
belittle other people's fame and dignity. At times this has been
done by way of gossip, as in the Madrid of the Austrias, or
as in the verse of the eighteenth-century poet Juan Pablo
Forner:

> I ran down Pablo to Juan,
> ran down Juan to Pablo;
> they know it, so with me
> they are sent to the devil.
> Pablo heard me with pleasure
> and with pleasure Juan listened
> and they both urged me on,
> so how did I offend them?

I imagine that if these lines had been read by Juan and Pablo
they would both have reacted with the same indignation. What
does he mean, "How did he offend me?" His case was quite
different!

Villamediana was famous for his verses, for his loves, but
especially for his evil tongue. How the Madrileños enjoyed
quoting his satirical verses:

> How smart is Vergel when he goes out!
> He sparkles with diamonds!
> Diamonds that once belonged
> to his wife's lovers.[1]

Or in the nineteenth-century lines of Pérez Galdós: "The embellished malice of wit is pleasing and tasty to our palates, and you will never hear a person praised for honesty, intelligence, or some other quality without the immortal, well-bred Uncle Paco coming in at once with his implacable disparagement."

The society of café and club has always been a good setting for the cultivation of slander. As Marañón reveals:

> . . . The café-goer is among other things an inexhaustible spring of resentment. When the man in the street, full of cares, passes in front of one of those club windows or sidewalk cafés, he feels in his bones, with no need to look at those inside, the darts of resentment shot out by such men who vegetate, chewing the cud of their own sourness, about a little round table or standing before a vast window.

And this sort of thing proves so appetizing to the Spaniard that he calls speaking ill of someone "giving a flavor to the tongue."

Individuals and communities can equally be objects of slander. The proverb book of Spain is full of pejorative judgments on places, most of them rhyming, most of them born in neighboring localities. Sometimes the definition is general and abstract:

De Jaen ni hombre ni mujer, ni aire que venga de él (I want nothing from Jaen, not man nor woman nor even the wind)

---

[1] There is a nice pun in Spanish here which cannot be translated:
> Qué galán sale Vergel!
> con cintillos de diamantes!
> *diamantes* que fueron antes
> *de amantes* de su mujer.—Tr.

Hijos de Madrid uno bueno entre mil (Sons of Madrid, one
  good one in a thousand)
Antes marrano que murciano (Rather a pig than a Murcian)
Amigo de León tuyo te sea, y mio non (Friend from León, let
  him be yours and not mine)
Buena es Cuenca para ciegos (Cuenca's okay, for the blind)

As we see, whoever invented the proverb gives no reason for
his judgment, which is at once negative and absolute. But then
the Spaniard does not have to explain to anyone the reason for
his preferences or dislikes. It is enough that he should state
them.

In other cases the insult is more precise. The charge may be,
for instance, dirtiness . . .

Mallorca tierra porca (Majorca, filthy place) or *El Melero de
  Muel que vendia mas moscas que miel* (The honey-seller
  of Muel who sold more flies than honey)
  Vanity . . .
Avila de los grandes fueros, dónde estan tus caballeros? (Avila
  of the great privileges, where are your knights?)
Toledano, tonto y vano (Toledo man, silly and vain)
  Ignorance, stupidity . . .
Palencia la necia, quien te oye te desprecia (Stupid Palencia,
  he who hears you despises you)
Los amantes de Teruel, tonta ella y tonto él (The lovers of
  Teruel, she's a fool and so is he)
*La justicia de Peralvillo que ahorcado el hombre hacia la
  pesquisa* (Justice in Peralvillo; after the man was
  hanged he was still looking for evidence)
*El hidalgo de Fuenlabrada que vendió el caballo para comprar
  la cebada* (The hidalgo of Fuenlabrada who sold the
  horse to buy barley)
  Hypocrisy . . .
Qué haré en Madrid que ne sé mentir? (What shall I do in
  Madrid when I don't know how to lie?)
Cordobés, falso y cortés (Cordovan, false and courteous)
  Thievery . . .

Si de Jaca me escapa, más rico soy que el Papa (If I escape
from Jaca, I'm richer than the Pope)

*Alba de Tormes, buena de putas, mejor de ladrones, mira tu
capa donde la pones* (Alba de Tormes, good for whores,
better for thieves, mind where you put your cloak)

*Valladolid de los vinos agudos, entran los mozos vestidos y
salen desnudos* (Valladolid of the pungent wines, the
lads arrive clothed and leave naked)

Granadino, ladron fino (Granada man, fine thief) In Spanish
proverbs the honesty of the place can be easily compro-
mised by the rhyme. If an adjective ends in *ino,* one can
easily attach the adjective *fino* (fine) in conjunction
with a gangster or, in the feminine, a whore.

Prostitution is a profession to which the Spaniards refer with
delight when describing the women of other localities. Judging
by the proverbs, it might seem to an outsider that there is not
an honest woman in the whole peninsula, a notion that would
never occur to anyone using these proverbs. No one thinks that
others have the right to insult the people of his town; still less
could he imagine that the sum of all these criticisms gives a very
low idea of the morals of the Spanish people. This would imply
a collective conscience, the absence of which we have already
noted in previous chapters.

Often the stranger who is naïve enough to want to marry in
this or that place is warned:

De Cariñena, ni mujer ni burra buena (In Cariñena neither the
women nor the donkeys are good)

*En Valencia el aire es fuego, la tierra es agua, los hombres
mujeres, y las mujeres nada* (In Valencia the air is fire,
the earth water, the men women, and the women
nothing)

Es de Peñafiel? pues no te fies de él (He's from Penafiel? Don't
trust him then)

*Cartagena, monte pelado, mar sin pescado, mujeres sin ver-
guenza, niños mal criados* (Cartagena, bare mountains,

sea without fish, women without shame, badly brought
up children)

De Andujar, la que no es puta, es bruja (In Andujar, she who
is not a whore is a witch)

Badajoz tierra de Dios, andan los cornudos de dos en dos (In
Badajoz, God's country, the cuckolds walk two by two)

En Catalojas hay más putas que hojas (In Catalojas there are
more whores than leaves)

De Daroca, o puta o loca (In Doroca, either a whore or a
madwoman)

Las toledanas, putas tempranas (Toledo girls start whoring
early)

In this brief selection, Spanish provinces from east to west
and from north to south are represented. No region, however
praised, escapes derogation. It all depends on one's point of
view:

Buena es Granada, pero junto a Sevilla no vale nada (Granada
is good, but not worth a thing compared to Seville)
becomes for the Granadan, *Buena es Sevilla, pero junto
a Granada no es maravilla* (Seville is good, but nothing
wonderful compared to Granada).

Sometimes these animosities infect strangers who come to the
areas for their summer holidays. Visitors quickly identify themselves with local likes and dislikes. When I was a boy we used
to spend the summer at Blanes where the hatred for Lloret, the
neighboring village on the same Costa Brava, was so great that
when we sang "Marina" we never said *Playas las de Levante,
costas las de Lloret* (beaches of the Levante, shores of Lloret),
but *Playas las de Levante, costas las que lloré* (beaches of the
Levante, shores that I wept for), thus preserving the rhyme
without mentioning the rival.

In some cases proverbs or sayings arise from something that
happened to a place, an event which it has tried to forget and
which the neighboring places keep joyously alive. There is the
episode of the donkey braying in *Quixote*, for example, or the

time the mayor of San Pol de Mar tried to protect a beautiful sundial from the inclemencies of the weather by putting an awning over it, giving rise to the sarcastic question still popular today, "San Pol, what's the time?"

The simplest words in Spanish often have a twisted, almost shady meaning. Take, for instance, *prejuicio*. One does not have to be a philologist to interpret this word in its original sense: a previous interest which makes one's judgment less than impartial. But notice that in English this prejudice may be favorable. "I cannot be impartial because he is a friend of mine and therefore I am prejudiced." In Spain, on the contrary, the prejudice is *always* negative. "He is prejudiced" means he hates him *a priori*, never that he loves him in advance.

The Spaniard's natural defensiveness and mistrust have logically led him to surmise that one passes easily from being honorable and honest to being stupid. *Ingenuo*, which implies a beautiful display of frankness in an individual, becomes an insult, and *cándido*, which in English retains its original meaning of "sincere," suggests a poor soul, a booby, in Spanish. "Don't be a fool" may often be interpreted as "don't be honest—take advantage of the circumstances even if to do so is forbidden or immoral."

"Versatile" in other Latin languages and in English implies the ability to do several things, being conversant with or capable of performing various jobs. This is too much for the envious Spaniard. *Versátil* describes the man who goes from one job to another, but instead of doing them all well—how are we going to tolerate that?—he does them all badly. "Of fickle and inconstant nature," says the Spanish dictionary.

In most countries "responsible" means one who accounts for what he has done, who takes responsibility upon himself, who is, in short, the acknowledged author of a thing. In Spanish *responsable* automatically acquires a sinister, derogatory tone; the responsible man is the one connected with a failure, with a mistake. In this case as in others, the dictionary marks, in its two definitions of the word, the Spaniard's whole psychology. First comes the simple definition derived from the etymological origin—obligation to respond for a thing—then the shading which the Spaniard has given it: moral charge or obligation as the result of a mistake.

There is no news that circulates more quickly in Spain than slander. The Spanish word for a gossip is *correveidile*, literally "run to tell him." A symbolic word, one wonders how many Spaniards must have hurried to bear bad news for it to have acquired this meaning.

Miguel Mihura once asked me to get him the reviews in the German papers of a forthcoming work of his that was to be put on in Hanover. At that time I had a pupil from Hanover and it was very easy for me to obtain them. The critics did not praise him (the work had been *A media luz los tres*, given during a Spanish Theater Week directly after *La vida es sueño*, and the German is hardly the person to pass from Baroque to modern drama in twenty-four hours.)

Some days later Mihura rang me up and reproached me for forgetting my promise. I told him I had the criticisms in my possession, but since they were not very interesting and were negative in character, I had not thought it opportune to send them to him. There was a moment's hesitation at the other end of the line.

"You didn't send them to me because they're bad?"

"That's right, Miguel."

Another stupefied silence.

"What a man! How good you are! Other friends would have sought me out everywhere to tell me I'd been roasted." This was not an exaggeration. Ordinarily, there is no degree of laziness which can keep a "friend" from finding a man whom he can upset.

When at a theatrical first night there are three hundred people applauding at the fall of the curtain and three stamping as a sign of disapproval, those who go on to a café after the show enter with a smile on their lips. They do not wait to be asked how things went.—"Oh boy, terrific stamping. . . !" As Larra said: "I do not know what propensity humanity has for the misfortune of another, but I have noticed that the audience goes out more gaily and wittily, more smiling and talkative, after a performance that has been booed."

A first night allows the Spaniard a unique opportunity to correct the habitual author-spectator relationship in which, in a way, he sees himself in an inferior position. He, to be listening for an hour and a half to what someone else has written? We have seen how he hastens out in the intermission to judge in a few minutes what the author took months or sometimes years to write. But his satisfaction is greater if he can make his expression of disapproval reach the author directly and not through intermediaries. The whistling, the stamping in Spanish theaters is an example of this direct vengeance; the passive has become active, the spectator has answered voice with voice.

In some cases such almost satanic settlement of accounts cannot be made openly because circumstances do not allow a man to reveal himself as the author's enemy. Then oblique methods may be used, such as stamping while at the same time clapping —I have seen it myself—so that one can assist the detractors and still show oneself as an intimate friend of the author's; or using a form of praise with poisonous shades of meaning when greeting the author during intermission. The author is nervous. . . . The first act has ended without angry tumult, but he imagines a great coldness in the atmosphere, which heralds disaster. The "friend" appears in the doorway and cheers him up: "Look here . . . *I* like it!"

On one occasion the impresario of a Madrid theater tried to eliminate the possibility of failure on opening night by giving free tickets to men of letters who were keen on the theater. His order reached the box office after one stall had already been sold to a regular customer. The impresario regretted the exception but he allowed it.

There followed a tumult. Whistles, stamping, adverse shouts filled the theater. In the middle of the excited, noisy mob, one spectator turned around and said with an astonished look, "It's not so bad, gentlemen, not so bad as all that!"

He was the only one who had paid for his seat.

The violence of the response to a theatrical production is due to extra-literary reasons and does not normally occur in the case of the novel or the essay. The novelist or the philosopher does not gather people in a closed space to exhibit his intelligence to them, to show off by humiliating them. Furthermore, the dramatist in Spain is the only kind of writer for whom a half-success can be enough to let him live decently by his work. And to see glory and money won at the same time is more than Juan Español can bear—he has to avenge himself somehow. . . . And if he has not been able to attend the opening he can always solace himself with the unfavorable reception in the papers. The most merciless critic is the one with the most readers.

But let us understand: It is not that envy of writers is stronger or more widespread in Spain than elsewhere; writers simply air their grudges more easily, and slanderous phrases, being wittier, are more often repeated. There are always facile poets to let loose a quatrain as soon as the curtain has fallen on an adaptation of a classic comedy:

> What has the adapter done?
> extremely little,
> changed hath to has
> and taken the author's fees.

I have had to attend many banquets in honor of an author. I do not remember one where the compulsory panegyric has not been combined with an outrageous attack on other writers. After three or four admiring phrases, the speaker of the moment lowers his voice slightly and looks around him.

"So-and-so is like that and not like others." And he proceeds with ten minutes (often more than he has devoted to his homage) of censure and vituperation.

As an example of this kind of dinner we may take one described by Baroja. The invitation read: "This is the delightful and peaceful dinner we are giving in honor of our ingenious friend Don Pío Baroja. . . !":

> But . . . I remember that the banquet was pretty chaotic. There were few people enjoying themselves. Ortega y Munilla asked me if they were going to insult

the old writers who had been kind enough to come
(certain young writers would wonder why they had
chosen me to give a banquet to); Cavia grumbled,
Cornuty started to use the familiar *tu* to Galdós and
called him to account for I don't know what, and when
Sánchez Gerona went out he met a group of young
gentlemen who said the banquet was a banquet of
modernists and that all modernists are pederasts.

There would seem to be a certain justification in the Spanish
literary world for this kind of resentment. It is such a poor
world, there is so little to share, that the slice taken by one
leaves the rest hungry. But the tragic fact is that this human
envy on the part of the dispossessed is maintained with the
same or greater force by those on top. If material resentment
were the only explanation of literary envy, it would end at the
moment when the envier achieved material riches, a smart house
or fame; that is to say, it would end at the moment of his arrival.

But it is not so. Achieving what is coveted does not mean
attaining generosity as well. In no way does it put a stop to envy.
Let us listen to Menéndez Pidal:

The lack [of pressures in our historical curve] . . . is
usually on the part of the eminent man who despises
the masses and who refutes or envies another eminent
man. . . . Every outstanding individual envies the enterprise of his fellow, he does not want to cooperate with
it but to usurp it and ruin it, a passion which is certainly
very human, and all too Spanish.

The patriarch of Spanish letters is referring to the Cid. Yes,
the first historical literary figure to appear in our books was
already a victim of this gloomy Spanish sin. But the point is
that Rodrigo Díaz was not envied by the oppressed vassals, the
farm laborers, the soldiers who marched on foot while he went
on horseback. Those who envied him and therefore sought his
perdition were the knights of the court, the nobles, the princes
of Carrión.

Even the man who is for many the noblest and unhappiest of

Spanish writers, Miguel de Cervantes, used the prologue to the second part of *Quixote* to launch a tremendous shaft against the pompous Lope de Vega. Defending himself against the accusation that he had already attacked him in the first part, Cervantes said: "I am sorry they called me envious and defined for me, as I was an ignorant, just what is envy. . . . [This is] a complete mistake, for I adore the wit of such a man (Lope), admire his works and his continual virtuous occupation. . . ."

Lope de Vega's "continual virtuous occupation" consisted in keeping several mistresses even after entering the priesthood. All Madrid knew this, so that Cervantes' defense, modestly given, was full of terrible sarcasm.

And it was not enough for Lope, the great Lope, simply to enjoy his success, his money, prestige, fame. When he saw Cervantes setting out on his difficult path, he made a contemptuous reference to the "fool who praises Quixote."

Two centuries later, Zorrilla was to complain:

> God held me chained
> on foreign soil eleven years.
> I should have died expatriate
> had He not broken my chain.
> I believe in God; yes, in truth;
> I bowed my head before Him
> and waited with fortitude
> for death or liberty.
> And bound hand and foot
> by slander and by envy
> I felt the base goads
> wound me with perfidy.
> And, Pedro, they were not from foreigners,
> those who treacherously wounded me;
> Pedro, the poisoned darts
> came from here!

Here are some opinions of Pío Baroja's on his colleagues: "Gómez de la Serna has always seemed to me a man without wit, extremely insipid, a *sinsorgo* (scatterbrain), as they say in Bilbao." "That Gómez Carrillo was one of the classical snobs without a background who come from America." "Pedro Corominas was pretty heavy-going, physically and spiritually." At other times the criticism is still sourer, when it returns something in kind. A journalist once asked him with that amiable malice characteristic of the race, "Do you know what Rubén Darío says about you?" "No, what does he say?" "He says: 'Pío Baroja is a writer of much substance (literally, 'dough'). We all know he was a baker.' " "Bah, that doesn't offend me at all. I shall say of him: Rubén Darío is a writer who wields a good quill. We all know he is an Indian."

Baroja's criticisms continue, no less grave for being synthetic: "Blasco-Ibáñez [is] evidently a good novelist . . . but I find him boring: he is a conglomeration of vulgar perfections which are common traits, which suffocate me." "Palacio Valdés . . . gives me the impression from the first moment of a very vain man who enjoys his self-sufficiency with an air of false modesty." "This lack of ethical sensibility is the reason why the books of Galdós, sometimes despite great technical and literary perfection, are failures." "La Pardo Bazán never interested me as a woman or as a writer. As a woman she was disagreeably fat, and, as a writer, I have rarely been in a condition to feel as she did about the vernacular and language." "I have never felt great enthusiasm for the literature of Benavente: he seems rather cold and theoretical to me." "Unamuno was extraordinarily intransigent. He did not listen to people: thus everything he said had nothing but his own approval." "Solana's phraseology sounded stale to me and did not interest me much." "Cajal was nothing much as a philosopher of medicine. I do not believe his scientific ideas were very far-reaching." "Valle Inclán was not a nice-looking man, not by a long shot. . . . His opinions were not worth much to me." "Another writer who speaks in a pedantic manner as I see it is Salvador de Madariaga . . . a scholastic, sententious man who does not seem intelligent to me." But perhaps the most incredible of Baroja's criticisms is the one he used for Villaespesa, whom he accused of being a bad poet—because he had not returned some money Baroja had lent him.

We are talking of well-known writers, writers who know they

have achieved prestige, fame, a name. But this is not enough for them. For the height of the Spaniard is not measured by the level to which he stands but by how low he leaves the others. Unamuno says:

> Envy has spoiled and still spoils not a few talented Spaniards who without it would be fresh and fruitful. We all remember the famous simile of the greasy pole. There is at the bottom of our soul a certain propensity not to think we are rich except in proportion to how poor the rest are, a pose which must be extirpated.

This trait is so prevalent that it has been popularized in a little story which, if it makes people laugh, does so because they see their subconscious portrayed in it. It tells of a rich man who used to pay a night watchman to pass in front of his house on cold and rainy nights. When the rich man heard the heavy shoes paddling through the puddles and the watchman's heavy breathing as he tried to keep himself warm, he would snuggle down between the blankets with a contented smile. "How wet that man must be getting!"

Anyone who rises to eminence in Spain does so at his own risk. As soon as his head stands out above the rest they will begin to take aim at it, and his former friendly relationships will do nothing to protect him. Among Spanish proverbs there is one which offers a beautiful example of charity and gratitude: "For the teacher a dagger thrust."

Thoughts of what the outside world will say have never had much effect on Spaniards. When Echegaray obtained the Nobel Prize for literature, demonstrations and banquets were organized in Spain with enthusiasm and discipline. To celebrate his triumph? No. To condemn it and protest his reward. (Another group, probably ideological enemies of the foregoing, used all its strength to oppose the granting of the 1912 prize to Pérez Galdós.) I have no sympathy for Echegaray's work, but I wonder whether such an impressive display of disapproval could have occurred elsewhere. As an example of a contrary reaction we may take the French, who argue about all the aspects of human and eternal life in letters and articles in the papers but who will form a granite block of mutual praise when they go abroad. What does Sartre think of the Catholic writer Claudel? "A marvel." What does the Catholic Mauriac believe about the Communist Aragon? "A magnificent writer."

And what of the Spaniard abroad? Cela was asked in America, "What do you think of Gironella?" "Giro . . . who?" In time the latter repaid him in the same coin, so that foreigners ended up believing they were both bad. And when does this warfare come to an end? With death. *De mortuis nil nisi bonum* (speak no ill of the dead) is absolute truth in Spain. As soon as the enemy has disappeared—in a graphic phrase they say "He no longer casts a shadow"—a wealth of dithyrambs is poured out, signed, to one's great astonishment, by those who were his most stubborn detractors during his lifetime. It would be very nice to think that this was just Christian charity, but I am afraid the explanation lies elsewhere. Iriarte suspected it:

> You only admire the old authors, Becerra.
> Only praise, only applaud, poets departed.
> Allow me, my friend, not to try to please you in this;
> I don't esteem your vote so much that I'd die to obtain it.

Envy can disguise itself as something else for purposes of pretense. As local pride for instance, as in the case of Lope de Vega's knight of Olmedo, killed out of pure envy of his successes in bullfights and with the ladies. The knight recalls Fabia's warnings:

> He always tells me to guard myself against the envy
>   which follows me,
> and never to walk at night without good reason.
> But it cannot be true that Rodrigo envies me
> as today he owes his life to me;
> for this debt will not allow so noble a knight
> to forget it in no time.

But yes, it *is* forgotten by his enemy, Don Fernando:

> Do you know who I am?
> D. Fernando—the man from Olmedo,
> the matador of bulls,

> who comes with arrogance and folly
> to confront the men of Medina. . . .

He then has the knight killed by a servant.

At other times envy is disguised as patriotic pride. I was amazed to hear one of the most generous men in Madrid refer angrily and spitefully to some Americans who were near us eating with good appetite: "Now these people are here insulting us with their dollars." This happened before the coming of the air bases, that is to say before there could have been a political feeling of "invasion" in the foreigner's presence. It is simply that the Spaniard is annoyed by other people's wealth, and a gentleman drinking good champagne in a corner of the restaurant has already won the dislike of most of the diners, at whom he has not even directed a glance. "And what's more he despises us," someone may say.

One of the words which has passed from Spanish to all languages of the world is *guerrillero*, guerrilla fighter. What is a *guerrillero*? A man who makes his war personal because envy does not allow him to make it collective and to act under the unified command of someone he must respect and obey. Pride and envy here exist in perfect symbiosis. I know as much as he does, I am as patriotic as he is, why should I obey him? So the *guerrillero* makes war on his own account.

When someone rises in Spain he has an "enviable" fortune. Why enviable? Why must this feeling unite itself automatically to the proof of someone else's luck? No one explains it. It seems natural to all of us Spaniards that if there is someone above us he should bear the punishment for his audacity. He should have to be envied. And as in the case of intolerance, a product of pride, envy has become so normal in Spanish life that it is possible to talk of *Santa Envidia*, Holy Envy, if what one desires is something good.

Yes, it is not only a question of desiring the maximum but of refusing to let others have their minimum. I have heard, "This business of making love is so good that it should be forbidden to the poor." A joke, obviously, but how is such a thing born if the ground has not been fertilized?

Or take the case of competitive examinations. Everyone is convinced they are absurd, incredible, that they do nothing to prevent injustice but rather create resentments and hatreds which last a whole lifetime. Yet whenever some well-intentioned minister has tried to end them he has met with pitiless resistance. "Oh no! If I went through them, let the rest go through them."

Unamuno, the most Spanish of Spanish intellectuals, employed some of his best dialectic in trying to explain the heart of his countrymen. We have already seen his defense of pride, where he was both the definer and the defined. In the case of envy he was merely an observer, but a passionate observer since he felt all our sins to be on his conscience. Never has this sin been better described than when Joaquín's wife Antonia tries to convince him he should dedicate himself to scientific research so as to obtain his own fame and glory. Joaquín replies:

> "I can't, Antonia, I can't. His [Abel Sánchez'] successes keep me from sleeping, and I would not be able to work in peace. The vision of his marvelous pictures would interpose between my eyes and the microscope, and would not let me see except through him what others have not seen. I can't, I can't."

And in his desire to save all Spaniards from the stigma, Unamuno makes Joaquín not responsible for his envy:

> ". . . Why did God look with pleasure on Abel's offering and with disdain on Cain's?"
> "Perhaps because God already saw in Cain the future slayer of his brother, the envious one."
> "Then He must have made him envious, have given him a poisonous draught."
> ". . . Hasn't it occurred to you that if Cain had not killed Abel it would have been the latter who would have ended up killing his brother?"
> "And how can that occur to you?"
> "God loved Abel's sheep and Abel, the shepherd, found grace in the eyes of the Lord; but Cain, the farmer, his fruits of the earth did not please God, nor

did He have grace for Cain. The one who received grace, the favorite of God, was Abel . . . the one without grace was Cain. . . ."

"And how was Abel to blame for that?"

"Ah! but do you believe that the fortunate ones, the receivers of grace, the favorites, are not to blame? They are to blame for not concealing, as the disgrace it is, any gratuitous favor, any privilege not gained by a man's own merits, for not hiding that grace instead of boasting of it. For I have no doubt that Abel would rub his grace into Cain's nostrils, would provoke him with the smoke of his sheep sacrificed to God. Those who believe themselves just are a lot of arrogant men who are going to humiliate others by being ostentatious about their justice. Someone or other has said there is no greater scum than the honorable person. . . ."

SLOTH

_____

. . . Will the good M. Sans-délai be right, slothful reader (if
you have already got this far), will he be right in saying ill of
us and of our sloth? Will he return one of these days to visit our
homes? Let us leave this question until tomorrow as you will already be tired of reading today: if tomorrow or another day you
are not, as you usually are, too lazy to go back to the bookshop,
too lazy to pull out your purse, and too lazy to open your eyes
to look over the pages I still have to give you, I will tell you as
if I were telling myself that all this I see or know, and much
more about which I hold my tongue, has happened to me many
times under this influence, the result of climate and other causes,
losing for me more than one amorous conquest through laziness;
abandoning more than one claim already started and the hopes
of more than one job . . . not making, finally, through laziness,
a just and necessary visit to social acquaintances who could
have been very useful to me in the course of my life. I will
remind you that I rise at eleven and have a siesta; that like a
good Spaniard I spend seven or eight hours on end talking or
snoring, making myself an unwanted fifth leg to a café table; I
will add that when they close the café I drag myself slowly to
my conversation group (because of laziness I have no more
than one) and, smoking one cigarette after another and yawning
ceaselessly, midnight or one in the morning finds me stuck to a
seat; that I often do not sup from laziness and from laziness do
not go to bed; in short, beloved reader, I will tell you that on the
many occasions when I have been desperate in this life I never
hanged myself once, I was too lazy.

—LARRA, "Vuelva usted mañana"

"There are years when one's not up to anything."

THE Spaniard is aware of some of the deadly sins. Pride, for example, which he considers natural—like lust, a prerequisite for anyone who is *muy hombre* (very much a man). On the other hand, he hardly ever accepts the accusation of being avaricious or gluttonous or violent or, of course, envious, which would belie his pride. (Saying what one thinks of someone else is not a sin.)

The attitude to sloth is a little like that toward lust. Its hold on us is admitted and even exaggerated. No one is ashamed of getting up late; on the contrary, one hears about the man who rises at eight in the "early morning," "with the milkman." When someone is told this he may easily remark in feigned surprise, "But is it light at that hour of the day?" And we boast of the siesta, even those of us who have no time to enjoy it.

It is said of Unamuno, here once again the most acute recorder of Spanish defects and virtues, that he answered a gentleman who was scandalized because the writer slept nine hours a day, "But don't forget that when I wake up, I am more awake than you."

The Spaniard, when he can, leans against a wall or a lamp post, a fact Julio Camba noticed when a foreigner used it to distinguish photographs taken in the streets of Spain from those of other countries.

It is not by chance that there are so many stories of Spaniards who declared eternal hatred for work and that so many comic writers—Alvarez Quintero, Arniches, Muñoz-Seca—have obtained a sure burst of laughter by putting the sluggard on the boards.

> *What they serve you in the stew*
> *has already paid duty ten times.*

Through laziness, many people let themselves be wittingly deceived. The institution of "paying duty" is an example. If a cook goes to the market she "pays more" than if the lady of the house goes in her stead, and there is no deceit whatever in her attitude. Everyone knows that she will find prices for meat and vegetables to be higher than the real ones. The difference, which she pockets, is the "duty"; it makes up for the money she has not received as wages.

Her mistress often resigns herself to this special tax as it allows her to sleep later in the morning, but this attitude is not exclusively feminine or modern. Sloth, here as on other occasions, is joined with pride, and it is difficult to say where one ends and the other begins. Sending a bellboy to the other side of the street to buy something can probably be equally ascribed to a wish to save oneself trouble and to the sensation of lordship that comes with ordering one's fellow around.

The custom is so old in Spain. Many administrators of rural and urban estates in the country have enriched themselves because their masters never bothered to look at their accounts; when it was not too late it was too early, and if not too hot it was too cold.

Work is bad for a man; the proof is that it is tiring, maintained González Ruano. And tiredness is something the Spaniard loathes so much that when one suffers from unrequited love he says, with an expression of ferocious torment, that he is "fatigued" (*pasa fatigas*, in the sense of "having a bad time").

There is a multitude of anecdotes about Spanish laziness, such as the one about the man who lost an eye because a drop of water kept falling on it and he did not want to move; or the one about the unemployed laborer who—after having complained about having no income—was offered a job and replied indignantly, "But man, there are three thousand of us here asking for work and you have to choose me?"

And a story said to be true tells of an Andalusian diver who was taking such a long time to clean the bottom of a ship that the foreman became intrigued and went down unexpectedly one day to find him asleep at the bottom of the sea, perfectly insulated from the noise of the world.

For many Spaniards work would be all right if it were at a level commensurate with their social standing. This level is nearly always very high, especially when it comes to accepting anything so humiliating as working with the hands. When Alonso de Contreras goes to work in a silversmith's shop and his boss sends him for water, the new employee says he is there to learn a craft, not to act as a servant, and throws the jug at his employer's head.

In the eighteenth century Charles III issued a decree stating that manual labor was not at variance with nobility and that its performance constituted no barrier to becoming, for example, a marquis. It did no good at all. Men continued to use a "social" excuse to reinforce their natural laziness. I work as a carpenter? I?

The origin of work is the biblical curse. This truth has never been so evident as in Spain, a country where the individual, however low his birth, however poor the surroundings in which he grew up, does not look on work as a logical condition of his existence but as a savage sentence which he must serve through no fault of his own. Every time the Spaniard gets up to go to the office or the workshop he is doing himself a profound violence. The eight hours he spends there are hours of purgatory. So it is not strange that he tries to shorten them by unhurriedly lighting a cigarette or escaping for a cup of coffee.

The Spanish verb *trabajar*, "to work," is often used for activities which in other countries are considered amusement. For example, *trabajar* on the stage is "to play."

"Routine," which in other languages signifies simply the work one does every day, whether pleasant or humdrum, in Spanish always means the work one does without interest or affection. And let us not forget that the Spanish word *mañana*, used to mean "leave for tomorrow what is urgent today," has passed into all languages. The meaning of *luego*, which up to the seventeenth century was "Soon! At once!" gradually relaxed in accordance with the way Spaniards used it until today it means "later," "afterward."

Many workmen in Spain have asked me about my experiences in the U.S.A. How was the worker treated there? When I talked to them of the wages and the opportunities in America, of refrigerators, cars, central heating, hot water, good roads, television, they gaped, stared at each other, nudged one another: "You see? That's how a man should work!" "That's a bit of all right," "That's the way to be a respectable person. . . ."

The trouble came when I began to describe the life of the American workman at work; most of them, I pointed out, could not smoke in the factory. "What's that—they can't light a fag? But how is that possible?"

"Because it is. Oh, and in many factories they count the minutes when you go to the toilet. . . ."

"What!"—this really seemed incredible to them—"Are you pulling our legs?" How could a firm intervene in something as personal, as individual as that? What slavery! And out would come the phrase so often repeated in Spain whenever one talks of punctuality, of strict attendance to duty, of keeping to the rules: "But that's not being men! That's being machines!"

Some years ago the Soviet Union, which has had no diplomatic relations with Spain since the Civil War of 1936–39, made a courteous gesture to the country. The children who had been taken to Russia by the Republicans were authorized to return to Spain. They were already men *de facto* and *de jure*, grown up and educated under a Communist regime; some of them even brought their Russian wives. Franco's Spain received them with a certain suspicion, but helped them to look for work and placed them according to the trade they had practiced in the U.S.S.R. In the factories they were sent to, there was a movement of curiosity and sympathy among the workers— nearly all of the Left—toward those who had come from what was nothing less than "the fatherland of the proletariat." But to the infinite astonishment of those who had expected moral and material help in the struggle for their claims (strikes are prohibited in Franco's Spain), the Russified Spaniards often reacted, against all Marxist logic, in favor of the employers. It was not that they had any special sympathy for them, but rather that in their idea of the division between capital and labor they saw the bosses as at least fulfilling their function as "exploiters," while the workers were not fulfilling theirs as "producers."

"But how dare you talk about claims?" shouted one of the newcomers; "why don't you start by dedicating yourselves to work, to making yourselves responsible at work? What way of looking after machines is that? What kind of eight-hour day do you think you're working? That's not producing, it's passing the time! In the U.S.S.R. you'd all have been sent to Siberia!"

For in the U.S.S.R., as in the U.S.A., work is a God before whom everybody bows. And it is not chance—not even the good fortune of great natural wealth—that has made these two the most powerful countries in the world.

In the meeting of Americans and Andalusians on the occasion of building the naval base at Rota in the south of Spain, it was as if two apparently sympathetic human groups were separated by an abyss of incomprehension. When an Andalusian heard that they were offering him so much money—a great deal more than he was used to—to work from nine to five, he only understood that he had to be there for those eight hours. For the American, on the other hand, it meant that he had to work all those eight hours. Surprise succeeded surprise. I heard a driver complaining in a Cadiz tavern:

"I get to the wharf with my truck. . . . I leave it to be loaded and go to the bar for a drink, that's natural isn't it? Okay, then up comes a Yankee who can jabber Spanish and says: Aren't you working as a driver? What are you doing here? Having a drink, I say, would you like to join me? And this nuisance answers, It's not the time for drinks but for work.—But what do you want me to do while they load my truck? And this guy says: Find yourself another and take it to the station. And so it went on all the morning, jumping from one truck to another like a cricket, without time for a coffee; that's not work, that's slavery."

Another grumbled about what he considered "dirty play" on the American's part. It seemed they had offered him work as a guard in an isolated part of the base, a job he was delighted to accept. But when the time to be paid arrived he found they had knocked off some hours. When he protested they showed him some photographs, taken from a helicopter, in which he was seen sound asleep, "during working hours," as the administrative man put it. This seemed very bad to the Spaniard, a breach of faith. (The fact that he really had been sleeping instead of watching as was his duty had very little importance. As we have seen, the Spaniard resents another's lack of confidence, even when there are all too many reasons for it.)

This Spaniard who wanted to be a guard is one of thousands who have known how to get a post, hold it officially and do very little in it. Most often they are doormen and attendants, and they especially thrive in public offices. They wear a gray uniform with gold on the cuffs and their mission is hard to explain to any society which believes in efficiency. Their most important function is *to be*, that is, to appear in a passage near a door, usually seated, to stand up respectfully when a superior passes, and, if he is of administrative rank, to open the door for him. They take papers and messages from one office to another and often bring up coffee from the street.

Their jobs are generally permanent, and from their corner they see the changing faces of ministers and undersecretaries, all the time smiling to themselves; they know that they will stay, while the man they salute obsequiously will be gone one of these days.

They are the fruit of others' pride—the desire to have someone to serve him—and of their own sloth. Barrera depicted the would-be office worker in the nineteenth century:

> Mother, I have a letter
> from Veremunda's son
> saying he has a safe job
> in a ministry;
> they give him eight thousand *reales*
> and the whole crowd
> of porters and attendants
> greet him respectfully.
> He gets up at eleven
> and goes to the office

and his only occupation
is to smoke by a stove
not far from a desk
where there are papers and pens.
Then he goes for a stroll,
then eats, then looks
in the café for his friends,
all of good family.

The situation remains largely unchanged today.

When the Spaniard has achieved his ambition of working at an office desk, he stops.[1] Any further progress is at the instigation of the state. This progress is according to "the roster," which shifts the employee slowly but surely on his upward way, generally requiring no effort on his part once he has passed the competitive examinations. His life is inexorably marked by bureaucracy; personal initiative has disappeared. Someone (God) or something (the state) is now looking after him.

But it is not only the state administration that in Spain has made a profession of sloth. The longing to be served, to have people to order around, is effectively linked with the Spaniard's desire to remain seated as long as possible. As an example, take the doormen of private houses whose mission, apart from a certain amount of cleaning and sporadic giving of information to anyone who asks for it, is simply to be there in case anything comes up. A porter performs his duty perfectly if he sits down on a chair at nine in the morning, after sweeping the doorway, and stands up at eleven at night to lock the door. His work is not to work. If one day he goes out to look for a taxi for a lady on the second floor who is about to have a baby, he has demonstrated the necessity for his presence for the next five years.

Or take the night watchman, who after opening doors for a while spends the rest of the night just staying by the fire, talking

[1] The word "ambitious," which in the United States often is a word of praise when applied to a man struggling to improve his and his family's position, is an insult in Spain. Why? Because an ambitious man's efforts oblige others to work harder. Because it means he is attempting to rise through evil arts, the only possible way in our country.

to someone who does not want to go to bed. Or the car attendant. Or the telephone lady, shut up in a little nook by the phone box, whose job is to give the right token to put in the slot and who sometimes looks after the washroom. Or the match seller who spends dead hours waiting for someone to want cigarettes who is not keen about going to the tobacconist's.

In short, there are innumerable occupations in Spain which involve being unoccupied for ninety per cent of the time in case they are needed for the other ten.

While such professions are to be found in most other countries, no where else are they so relished as in Spain.

It is not that the Spanish workman or employee is satisfied with his miserable wages. No, he seeks a way out of his situation. But the most direct way—to work hard to better his position—is too tiring; and besides, considering the country's economic circumstances it is pointless, "because there's nothing to do here." And so he seeks liberation through the gate of luck. This is the reason for the incomparable success of the Lottery, of the Pools—in which are combined two national passions, football and the dream of becoming rich—and of the Lottery of the Blind. These three are so perfectly stratified that all Spaniards may take part in them, from the one who has only a few cents to buy a ticket for the blind to the very rich man who buys several whole tickets in the Christmas Lottery, wagering thousands of pesetas to obtain millions.

(Curiously enough, this taste for the spin of fortune's wheel has not carried the Spaniard to the next logical step. I refer to the vice of gambling, which in Spain only attacks certain ladies who get bored in the afternoon and some gentlemen of extraordinary means. I do not believe governmental prohibition has had an effective influence here, as the Spaniard has resisted authority in so many other areas.)

The Spaniard who slaves at a job he does not fancy may not want to try for a better one, even if it requires less work. He wants the change to be brilliant, decisive and absolute, to make the leap from nothing to everything. Azorín describes such a case in *La Voluntad*: "A young priest who used to eat with us is protecting a blacksmith of this village who has invented nothing less—you may well wonder!—than an electric torpedo. This indeed is classically arch-Spanish—not study or work, not improving agriculture or trade, no. An electric torpedo which may make us owners in four days of all the seas of the globe."

Let us suppose that a man has no grand projects. He still wants to make the leap, and nearly always this desire leads him to competitive examinations for a state post. These examinations are for jobs available to those of all social levels—from postman, a job which anyone who has left primary school can seek, to positions which require a small degree (Bachelor, for customs) or a big one (a law degree, for notaries). The preparatory programs are diverse and the difficulties vary, but the principle behind them is always the same: the Spaniard sacrifices some years by working intensely, so that he may not have to work any more for the rest of his life. (If he does it will be on his own account and at his own risk.) His boss, the state, will normally require no more from him than going to the office for a few hours in the morning. In Madrid they tell the same anecdote about several ministries: a gentleman, trying to go upstairs to an official center, is detained at the door. "Where are you going?" asks the porter. "There's no one up there."

"Oh!" says the gentleman, surprised. "Don't they work in the afternoon?"

"It's in the morning they don't work. In the afternoon they don't come."

In principle every bureaucrat believes that after finishing his purgatory of examinations—and in view of the sweat and anguish they cause him the expression is not exaggerated—he is entitled to a paradise more like the Moslem one than the Christian. Whoever happens to require his services is therefore regarded with suspicion and annoyance which are only allayed when the bureaucrat can order him to correct his papers or buy more stamps.

When everything is in order he says, "Come back at the end of the week."

With a salary that is often paltry, the functionary considers the work to which he is submitted as something entirely disagreeable which can only be alleviated by bad manners. While one Spaniard goes up to an office window, seeing the state as an enemy with whom he must coexist, another Spaniard watching him approach from the other side is seeing him, at the very least, as someone who "raises problems." The idea that the government pays him precisely to help solve those problems does not appear to pass through the mind of any Spanish functionary, to such a point that the phrase "He has come to me with a form," that is to say with something to solve, is equivalent to "He has come to bore me stiff."

The situation is so clear and so widely accepted that no one thinks twice of a note such as the one a Madrid newspaper published on September 30, 1965. In it the Minister of Information was describing what had been agreed upon in the Cabinet, and in referring to the new regulations for public employees he said:

"The hours will be from nine to two and from five to half past seven. As you are aware, the Wages Law comes into force on October the first, and it is natural that the functionaries who start to receive the salaries that have been fixed should fulfill their task during the hours that have been laid down." In other words: "Look here, you no longer have an excuse for arriving late or for not going to the office. We have raised your salary and the least you can do is show up for work." That this work should be efficient, that the public waiting its turn at the office windows should be attended to as befits citizens who pay taxes so that these functionaries may receive their salary, is something quite different. Why should functionaries change their attitudes now, attitudes still almost the same as those held by the character in Pérez Galdós's novel *La de Bringas*, in which a boy of sixteen "never set foot in the office except to be paid the four hundred and sixteen reales and some odd cents that we [the Spaniards] gave him for his pretty face. . . . In the conceited brain of Rosalía Bringas the idea had become imbedded that the appointment was not a favor but the fulfillment of a duty of the State toward precocious Spaniards. . . ."

Miguel Mihura portrayed the Spanish functionary in a comedy called *Sublime decisión* which opened in Madrid in 1955. The play was set at the beginning of the century, but nobody missed the point of the similarity between the situation portrayed and what they saw every day. The scene represented the inside of a government office. On the right was a little window which a taxpayer approached timidly. The audience neither saw nor heard him but his presence was implied in the words of the functionary. "What's wrong with you? Yes sir, here is where these documents are handed in. But this is not the time for handing them in. The time is when we're shut. You don't understand? Then you're an idiot!"

"When I was a functionary," said another character, "I always held a stick in my hand. And the first one who showed his head, bam! a good whack. . . . And so I never even had to speak!"

The great cartoonist Mingote has represented dozens of times the type of public official who has no sympathy for the man who stands queued up minute after minute. This official, who often works in a place where there is no information service, tells a man who has been in line for half an hour that a certain stamp is missing from his application, a stamp which he has to go and fetch and lose his turn unless the attendant helps him get it after receiving a tip. I am sure that if someone proposed to such government officials, "Why don't you put up some placards telling people about all the documents and stamps they need before they queue up?" they would start in astonishment. Why? Let him find out if he likes and if not let him take the consequences. It would be a nice thing if we had to act as nursemaids to people who haven't got their wits about them!

This strange conception of the official's mission—that he has a post which is a gift from Providence and therefore requires no effort on his part—probably has historical roots. The enlargement of the administrative services dates from the century of the great modern reforms, the nineteenth, when there were also frequent political changes. When a party rose to power it had to reward those whose efforts had assisted it, and the easiest way was to find room for them in the ministries. Although the ministries had been purged of supporters of the defeated party, there always remained some specialists who could not be thrown out, and the new chief had to solve the situation by creating new posts. Soon the political parties agreed that nobody should be moved, and so was born the concept of "acquired rights." What did the parties care, since the paying was to be done by someone else, an entity called the state? Public functionaries multiplied, but the idea of "functionary" was engraved much more deeply in their minds than the idea of "public." What did they owe the public if it had not appointed them? And when posts became obtainable by competitive examinations, the old attitude was retained, and exists today as it did then.

(Since the Civil War, and especially in the last ten years when Spain has opened up more to Europe and America, circumstances have partly changed. People, all the people, have begun to fancy a kind of life which hitherto was reserved for special groups at the top of the social scale. Therefore, since salaries were not sufficient and since the laxity of working hours permitted it, a system of working in several different places was initiated. Double work is today normal for many Spaniards, and there are even those who have three or four jobs; this, however, does not improve their efficiency. Why should they be efficient if what they are paid for any one of their jobs is not enough to oblige them to be?)

When a Spaniard has to confront the state and its tentacular arms, he never does it suddenly, for he knows that he would be smothered during months and months of desperate struggle. There are two comfortable ways for him to go about it. One is to flatter the functionary's pride with the name of a common friend, preferably an important name. Then he will see the obstacles sink, the barriers disappear, the rocks vanish which lay in his path. The most important papers can be obtained in ten minutes along with smiles, tobacco, and slaps on the back.

One of the reasons why the bureaucratic service does not improve in Spain is precisely because those who have money, name, political connections, those who might complain effectively of their treatment at the office windows, do not go near them, preferring to use the roundabout method described above. And so the only ones who do present themselves are people of less importance, who can easily be humiliated without consequences. If someone important stands in line with the crowd—either through humility or ignorance—and then complains of his treatment, the employee hastens to explain, "If we had only known it was you! Why didn't you tell us. . . ?"

Spanish sloth has created the greatest system of intermediaries in the world. What is an intermediary? The man who does the work someone else does not feel like doing. There are intermediaries for all tastes and all social classes. For instance, the *habilitado* of the public functionaries, a métier I have tried to explain many times to foreigners. . . .

"But what does this man do?"

"He collects my pay from the state."

"And what does he earn from that?"

"A commission I give him."

"But why can't you get your pay directly?"

"It's very complicated, you have to go to the treasurer's office, queue up—it's not worth it, so I let him do it. . . ."

Faced with bureaucratic red tape the Spaniard retreats and lets a specialist act on his behalf. This applies for any negotiation of an official type. You have to take out an affidavit that you have never been convicted, a birth or baptismal certificate, a passport? The Spaniard does not go to the Ministry of Justice, to his municipal office, to his parish priest, to the Ministry of Government. He goes to an agency which takes charge of the matter. The intermediary exists both for the important and the trivial. If you pause for a moment to look up the street, a boy or an old man arises from the ground and asks you respectfully if you want a taxi. If you do he places himself a few steps higher up the street in an attitude of ambush and, as soon as he sees the green light indicating an empty cab, waves frantically and screams.

When the taxi stops by you, he opens the door with a smile,

breathing heavily to show what it has cost him to secure it: "Well sir, we've been lucky." And if he has a peaked cap, an important accessory for a good intermediary, he takes it off respectfully to receive the tip. The Spaniard gets majestically into the cab, converted into a person of importance by a couple of pesetas.

There are intermediaries in all establishments, however modest. The barber has a boy who brings the water or the clean towels, and in the cafés there is a tobacco seller, a lady for the washbasins, and another in charge of the telephone. Each has his special function of making things easy for the customer. And if this is so for normal conveniences, we can imagine what happens when there are particular difficulties in obtaining something. The intermediary then is not just a help but simply the only chance. I remember when there used to be problems in obtaining railway tickets; a worried foreigner told me what had happened to him:

"I've been three days trying to get to Madrid," he said in Barcelona, "three days without managing it."

"What have you done to get a ticket?"

"What could I do? Queued up at the booking office for hours, but when I got there there were no seats left."

"At the booking office? But good God, man! For tickets you have to go to the bar on the corner."

The poor man could not understand it.

To be an intermediary it is not necessary to be paid, to have a job, or to be available for hire. There are those who do it in order to give the impression of working but without tiring themselves. Thus in the world of Spanish cinema there is a type of gentleman whose function is simply to tell people something which is going to happen to them. For example, the actor Fernando Fernán-Gómez told me that a friend often comes up to him: "I say, has So-and-so rung you up? No? Well he will. He told me to tell you."

All that day and even through the week this message is repeated continually, by different people. Then the messenger meets "So-and-so" and tells him he has already told Fernán-Gómez that he is going to ring him.

The cinema industry has been a great refuge for loafers because, like the world of letters, it allows a man to spend months, without causing notice, preparing some work; even taking a stroll in the street can be "capturing the atmosphere."

It is evident that laziness is a science to which time and study must be devoted. Meal times in Spain are a classic example: late rising produces a late breakfast; after that lunch and naturally dinner are put off as long as possible. The person who is in bed does not feel like getting up, the one having an apéritif with his friends sees no reason for interrupting the pleasant moment, the one arguing in a café sees no need to go to bed. . . .

There is no doubt that the ascendency of the café in Spain is due to the Spaniard's special conditioning, which enables him to sit on a sofa for hours and hours, watching or talking. Sloth also helps explain the popularity of the clubs, where grave gentlemen live watching people in the street, and of the sidewalk cafés. An American journalist said of Madrid that it gave him the impression of a city divided into two groups. The first sit in the sidewalk cafés watching those who circulate, and the second circulate while watching those seated in the cafés.

It is not surprising that at a café sport—billiards—the Spaniards should have led the world for so many years.

Sloth needs an alibi, however. It may be . . . the heat (Who's going to work in this heat!) or the cold. It may be rheumatism, it may be the lack of family understanding which makes everything difficult, as in the case of the Andalusian youth who after many months of unemployment told his mother he was beginning a job next day. "Where?" asked his mother hopefully.

"At the excavations."

"At the excavations? So far away?"

"Is it so far? Well, I shan't go then."

Lack of money is not enough to move the authentically lazy man. If someone reminds him how easy it is to earn money by moving himself, he says it is not worth it: "No one gets anything here, Spain is very bad for that." This is like the exclamation of Don Periquito's which so irritated Larra. Abandoned, idle and slovenly, he explained: "There's nothing to do in this country." Must his room then look like a lion's den? "—What do you expect in this country!" He remained quite satisfied with this excuse.

Spanish houses are generally uncomfortable, partly for economic reasons, as we have seen, partly because it is easier to go to the café than to try to make them comfortable. I shall always remember a lady in Cordova whom we called on when the hotel we had tried could not offer us a room. The lady showed us the bedroom she let to strangers, and when I tried the bed I found it very hard. I told her so and she was surprised at my pretensions. "We all know," she said seriously, "that you sleep badly when you're traveling."

Nevertheless, Spanish houses have inducements to sloth which are not found in other richer countries. For example, the elevator is now an essential feature for five-story buildings in any popular Spanish district, while in prosperous West Germany, people must still use the stairs, even in buildings constructed since the war. The same holds true for central heating, which is relatively more widespread in Spain than in France, Germany, or England.

Every Spaniard, however humble, reckons he has a right to vacations away from home; many wealthier people in New York have never enjoyed the kind of vacation that seems quite natural to a poor dressmaker or concierge in Madrid or Barcelona.

The Spaniard's general objective is to get money without working, "without doing a stroke." This objective has become so pronounced that professional swindlers today work incredibly hard at their pitches in order to make a living. I have been taken in a couple of times by confidence men, and have admired the mental effort required to invent the story with which they hoped to get a few pesetas out of me; the amount has always been out of all proportion to the effort.

But there was a man in Spain who managed to be paid for

doing virtually nothing. Only in Spain could one find Don Tancredo, who used to go out into the bullring covered with flour, place himself on a pedestal and pray to God, so that the bull, when let out, would in fact believe he was a statue and not gore him. Don Tancredo was paid for keeping still, and thus his name serves as a symbol of perfectly achieved ambition. "Ah yes," a Spaniard will say admiringly. "He does the Don Tancredo bit. . . ."

Spaniards have mental pigeonholes for opinions on various subjects. These pigeonholes are filled with superficial information placed there without thought of contrast, comparison, or reliability. It is enough that the information fill some gap; with that the Spaniard's position can be decided with regard to a certain actor, a certain literary figure:

> Scanty ideas passed through the Spaniard's brain like the Civil Guards, in pairs. Here no more than two things were conceived: black or white, great or small. And if anyone attempted to introduce a third notion, the idea of a shade of meaning, that of a just mean between the simple symmetry of the pairs, *anathema sit*. Sagasta and Canovas, Calvo and Vico, Lagartijo and Frascuelo. . . .

Manuel Machado is speaking, and, although he does not say so, the intellectual laziness he describes is partly a function of envy. For in presupposing a pair there is always the satisfaction of attacking someone, the bad one; thus one mitigates the disgust at having to praise the other.

Once declared, this admiration or hatred is valid forever and is absolute, without one modification. If Cervantes is a literary genius he has also to be perfect in every other sphere of life, and his admirers take it as a personal insult if someone notes that the great writer was perhaps not completely scrupulous in his administration of the state's goods. Baroja's admirers do not admit that their idol's style was grammatically defective, and if you show them patent examples they say that Baroja "has the style of not having a style," or something like that. All is granite, immutable.

In this long-term maintenance of an opinion, pride doubtless plays as important a role—already referred to as "maintaining and not modifying"—as sloth. Why should one restudy the thing and at worst have to change his opinion?

Such precision in ignorance occurs in every aspect of intellectual comprehension. For example, why should we make the effort to study a foreigner thoroughly if we get along all right with a cliché definition for each country? We all know the German is heavy but disciplined and hard-working—just see how Germany has risen again. The Italian "is intelligent, but frivolous and cowardly in war"; the Frenchman "is always deceived by his wife and hates Spaniards"; the Englishman "is boring and very hypocritical"; the American "is childish and not very cultured. . . ."

The same goes for regional descriptions: "The Catalan is serious and hard-working, but how he talks!"; "The Aragonese is stubborn"; "The Basque eats a great deal. . . ." As the song says:

> If you want to be happy as you tell me,
> don't analyze, lad, don't analyze . . .

This mental laziness explains much in Spanish politics over the years. Programs calling for a united effort by the citizens are never popular; the people much prefer, on a national scale, politicians who promise them happiness without excessive effort on their part, the miracle workers in short. In 1931, describing the Republic as a nation "of workers of all classes" did not arouse enthusiasm among a people who had fought and seen loved ones die for such unrealizable myths as Anarchism, the Empire, the worker's paradise, or a return to the Spain of St. Teresa.

Nor does the Spaniard, in his daily life, help himself so that others may help him. Unlike other countries, Spain has extremely few citizen groups which meet to organize their district, their school, or their public health before asking for government help. The Spaniard expects the help to come first. If not from heaven, at least from the state, which exists for that purpose. A popular song reminds him:

> Do you want to live without care?
> Let things take their course
> and what God sends you
> will come into your hands.

There is something else which obviously aids the laziness of many Spaniards, the same thing that has made many Arab cities—with their narrow streets, veiled women, religious fanaticism, open air markets, traditional craftsmanship—appear just the same today as in the Middle Ages. It is something which is at odds with progress, because progress implies an attempt to cooperate with changing times and, if necessary, to twist the "natural" course of events. It is called fatalism, and under its protection men refuse to move because they are convinced of the uselessness of their efforts. "To the man who's enrolled among the poor, it's all the same whether he runs or sits."

The will of Allah has been converted into the will of the Christian God, or perhaps rather into that of an abstract entity called Destiny, Fate, Fatality. One of the works most appreciated by the public of the romantic age was *Don Alvaro or the Force of Destiny*; the author was the Duke of Rivas, and millions outside of Spain know the plot from Verdi's opera *La forza del destino*. Don Alvaro loves Leonor, the daughter of the Marquis of Vargas, who opposes the match; when Don Alvaro is about to carry her off he is surprised by the Marquis. He throws a pistol on the floor in token of surrender, and the weapon goes off and kills his beloved's father. In the confusion which follows, Don Alvaro believes that she too has died, and goes off to the Italian war to seek death. There he meets a brother of Leonor's, eager for revenge. He tries not to make any more "Vargas blood" flow, but is obliged by the other's insults to fight him, and wounds him mortally. Condemned to death, he resigns himself to his fate, but an enemy attack allows him to escape. He flees and takes refuge in a monastery, and there another of the Marquis' sons comes to seek him out. Once again Don Alvaro tries to avoid a duel, and once again he is provoked until it is impossible not to fight. He wounds this brother as well, who asks for a confessor. Don Alvaro goes to fetch a monk who lives as a penitent in a hermitage. The "monk" turns out to be his beloved, who has been taking refuge there for years to expiate her part in the family misfortunes. When the dying man sees his sister he believes she has been living in the monastery with Don Alvaro, calls her to his side, and, before dying, stabs her with a dagger. Alvaro, maddened, insults the monks who arrive terrified on the scene, proclaims himself the devil, and commits suicide by throwing himself over a precipice. We have to recognize that his act, however desperate it may have been, answers to a certain logic. If there was anyone who could speak of bad luck and fatalism it was, without a doubt, Don Alvaro.

Without quite this dramatic quality, a fatalistic attitude is shared by many Spaniards, perhaps from the subconscious need to find a pretext for their scanty desire to work. For if, as it is written, "He who is born for the eighth part shall never attain the quarter," it is obviously absurd to tire oneself in vain.

This philosophy leads gifted men to renounce both material and moral glory beforehand. Blossoming writers refuse to write. "In any case the censorship's going to prohibit it," they growl; "Here you can't do anything"—with which their conscience remains perfectly tranquil. It is useless to try to encourage them by reminding them that, even supposing their work is prohibited—and you never know what may happen when it is finished—they will be left with all of Latin America and with translation into other languages as roads which could lead them to fame. They remain unconvinced. They shake their heads sadly, several times: "Nothing, there's nothing to do. . . ."

And so another *Don Quixote* remains unwritten. Yes, destiny stands for much in the daily life of the Spaniard. It is significant that when he is offered a new post in the civil service, in the army, in the navy, he calls it *destino* (meaning both "appoint-ment" and "fate").

And when he stops working, he is given a pension (*le jubilan*). *Jubilar*, according to the dictionary, means "to exempt a functionary from service because of age or sickness"; its other meaning is "to give shouts of joy."

⚞ *Epilogue* ⚟

YES, Spain is different. Perhaps because of its geographical position. For what is Spain by nature, the tail of Europe or the head of Africa? The Frenchman's remark that Africa begins at the Pyrenees is untrue, but the man who says that the Europe represented by what is French, German, Flemish, Scandinavian, really begins at Gibraltar is not quite right either. Spain has always vacillated between a call from above and a call from below, between the North and the South. This hesitant shifting, which has depended sometimes on the difference between what the country feels and what suits it, has given it, on the one hand, its continuous lack of political stability, and on the other, its tremendous individuality.

In a way this Spanish vacillation is similar to that felt by a nation situated on the other side of Europe. Russia, like Spain, sits between two worlds which pull her in opposite directions. In her case, the European influence is opposed by the influence of Asia. The Russians, similar to the Spaniards in many respects (living in a hostile environment with great meterological changes; possessing a feeling for music, an innate hospitality, an exacerbated patriotism, mysticism; exhibiting violence in revolutions) historically look at Europe both with admiration and with fear of losing their personality should that influence become excessive.

I am reminded of a significant episode which took place in the nineteenth century. The new invention of the railway had spread all over the continent. Writers and politicians extolled the new system of transport as the bond which Europeans of different countries had long needed in order to know and understand one another better. All the nations signed treaties allowing the rails to cross their frontiers—all except Russia and

Spain who, without actually agreeing, saw in the hand held out to them both the possibility of greater trade and the threat of invasion. Both had suffered at the hands of the same reorganizer of Europe, Napoleon. After many hesitations they were eventually to agree to collaborate in the railway system, but their old misgivings were to be manifested in the actual dimensions of the tracks, which in both Russia and Spain are wider than those throughout the rest of Europe. The idea seems to have been the same in both cases: unanimity . . . with certain precautions.

Through the seven touchstones of the Deadly Sins, I have tried to describe the average Spaniard. A sin cannot be said to have any virtue in itself, in spite of the adjective "holy" which Spaniards absurdly apply to envy and anger, but some sins can produce positive values.

Pride, for example, gave birth to Don Quixote, who wanted— all by himself—to clean up his country of evildoers and enchanters; and, in broader terms, pride has been the mother of a characteristic which foreigners have admired in Spain for many years. I refer to dignity, that unique way the Spaniard has of appearing to be standing up even when on his knees, well-dressed when naked, well-fed when hunger is gnawing. It is the quality which enables the poorest of Spaniards to show twice the gratitude for the gift of a cigarette or a glass of wine as for a handsome tip. For smoking or drinking together implies an equality much more important than money. And the Spaniard's individualism, which does so much harm to the organization of his country, produces on the other hand a human type unique in the world, as different from neighbor to neighbor as Spaniards themselves are different from other Europeans.

Lust has given the world two Spanish literary types, Don Juan and La Celestina, and a series of popular verses in which complete love stories are beautifully summarized in three or four lines.

From anger comes the bravery and daring of men who crossed the Alps and Andes, deserts of New Mexico and swamps of Flanders; who in this attempt to prove their manhood left Spanish names and customs in twenty-five countries.

In the lee of sloth comes the café conversationalist, whose spark, whose wit has shadings not to be met with in any other country in the world. (Unamuno declared that Spanish culture is to be found more in the cafés than in the universities.) It is in the Spanish café that the conversation is enough to fill interesting hours without any need to resort to alcohol or drugs, with gluttony amplifying this euphoria with the well-served table.

There is only one sin where I find it difficult to cite a positive value. I refer to envy, which in Spain does not even serve, as elsewhere, to mobilize human energies in an attempt to outdo the envied person. For the Spaniard it is easier simply to speak ill of him and bring him down a peg.

Rereading these pages, I get the impression that the way to improve the Spaniard can be summed up in a possibility as simple as it is revolutionary.

If from time to time, only from time to time, we were to believe that the other man might be right. . . .

And if this belief did not automatically make him odious . . .

I believe that would be enough.

Bibliography

AUTHORS MENTIONED OR QUOTED

ALARCÓN, PEDRO ANTONIO DE — (1833–1891) Writer and politician. *El niño de la bola, El sombrero de tres picos, El escándalo*, etc. Also wrote travel books.

ALARCÓN, JUAN RUIZ DE — (1580?–1639) Dramatist, born in Mexico; a leading representative of the Golden Age. Associated with Tirso de Molina. *El semejante de si mismo, La verdad sospechosa, Ganar amigos*, etc.

ARNICHES, CARLOS — (1866–1943) Famous playwright; specialist in the "madrileño sense of humor." *El pobre Valbuena, Es mi hombre, Alma de Dios*, etc.

BAREA, ARTURO — (1897–1957) Republican writer, fled to exile after Franco's victory. Chief work *La forja de un rebelde* (novel); also wrote autobiography and history. Nationalized English.

BAROJA, PÍO — (1872–1956) Village doctor, baker, prolific novelist and essayist. *Vidas sombrías, Zalacaín el aventurero, La dama errante, Paradox Rey, Mala hierba, Aurora roja, Casi nada, Las inquietudes de Shanti-Andia*, etc.

BARRERA, P. M. — Nineteenth-century author. *Dos cuadernos, Cuadros sociales y composiciones diversas Madrid 1868*.

BÉCQUER, GUSTAVO ADOLFO — (1836–1870) One of the purest romantics. *Leyendas Españolas, Desde mi celda, Rimas*, etc. An extraordinary poet in prose and verse.

BENAVENTE, JACINTO — (1866–1954) Famous contemporary playwright. *Los intereses creados, Lo cursi*, etc. Elected Deputy to the Cortes for Madrid. Nobel Prize winner.

BLASCO-IBAÑEZ, VICENTE — (1867–1928) Internationally popular novelist. *La barraca, Arroz y tartana, Sangre y arena, Los cuatro jinetes del Apocalipsis*.

CADALSO, JOSÉ DE — (1741–1782) Preromantic in poetry, satirical observer in prose works. *Cartas marruecas, Eruditos a la violeta*, etc.

CALDERÓN DE LA BARCA, PEDRO — (1600–1681) Dramatist, extraordinary poet of the Spanish Baroque. *Autos sacramentales* and other religious works. Plays of customs (*El alcalde de Zalamea, La dama duende*) and philosophical plays (*La vida es sueño*). "Calderonian husband" is a Spanish phrase denoting the jealous ones he portrayed in *El mayor monstruo los celos*; *A secreto agravio, secreta venganza*; *El médico de su honra, el pintor de su deshonra*; etc.—husbands who shed blood in defense of honor.

CAMBA, JULIO — (1882–1962) Humorist, travel journalist. *La rana viajera*; *Sobre casi todo, sobre casi nada*; *La casa de Lúculo o el arte de bien comer*; etc.

CASTELAR, EMILIO — (1832–1899) Parliamentary orator on the Republican side, of great prestige. *Historia de Europa, El siglo XIX, Lucano* (novel), *Discursos académicos*, etc.

CASTRO, AMÉRICO — (1885–   ) Professor; living in U.S. since the Spanish civil war. Great renown in the field of history (*La realidad histórica de España*) and in that of literature (*El pensamiento de Cervantes, Don Juan en la literatura española, Santa Teresa y otros ensayos*, etc.

CASTRO, GUILLÉN DE — (1569–1631) Playwright. *Las mocedades del Cid* and *Hazañas del Cid* are his best-known works, imitated by Corneille in *Le Cid*.

CELA, CAMILO JOSÉ — (1916–   ) Novelist who initiated "tremendismo" with *La familia de Pascual Darte, Viaje a la Alcarria, Nuevas andanzas de Lazarillo de Tormes*, etc.

CERVANTES, MIGUEL DE — (1547–1616) Author of the best and most famous Spanish novel, *El ingenioso hidalgo Don Quijote de la Mancha*. First part 1605, second 1615. Plays (*Ocho comedias*). Short novels (*Novelas ejemplares*), etc.

CONTRERAS, ALONSO DE — (1582–1633) Soldier, author of an autobiography, *Vida del capitán Alonso de Contreras*.

DARÍO, RUBÉN — (1867–1916) Inspired Latin American poet, author of *Azul, Los raros, Rimas*, etc.

DONOSO-CORTÉS, JUAN — (1809–1853) Writer and statesman, conservative in spirit.

ECHEGARAY Y EIZAGUIRRE, JOSÉ — (1832–1916) Poet, playwright, economist, mathematician and politician. In 1904 shared the Nobel Prize for literature with the poet Mistral. *El gran galeoto, O locura o santidad, En el seno de la muerte*, etc.

ESPRONCEDA, JOSÉ DE — (1808–1842) As romantic in his life as in his work; sings of the rebel and was one. "El estudiante de Salamanca," "El pirata," "El canto del cosaco" (Hurrah, cossacks of the desert, hurrah) celebrating violence, pillage and rape, "El verdugo," "El mendigo," etc.

FERNÁNDEZ FLÓREZ, WENCESLAO — (1886–1963) Humorist, keen critic of old Spanish customs. *El secreto de Barba Azul*; *Las siete columnas*; *Relato inmoral*; *El malvado Carabel*; *El toro, el torero y el gato*; etc.

FORNER, JUAN PABLO — (1756–1797) Spanish magistrate and poet.

FOXA, AGUSTÍN DE — (1903–1958) Diplomat, poet, playwright, novelist, famous author of bon mots. *El almendro y la espada* (poetry), *Baile en Capitanía, Cui-Pin-Sing* (plays), *Madrid de corte a cheka* (novel), etc.

GARCÍA GÓMEZ, EMILIO — (1905–   ) Professor; ambassador; author. The best Arabic specialist today. *El collar de la paloma, Poemas arabigo andaluces*, etc.

GIRONELLA, JOSÉ MARÍA — (1917–   ) Novelist, author of *Los cipreses creen en Dios*, about the prelude to the Spanish civil war, and *Un millón de muertos*, about that contest.

GÓMEZ DE LA SERNA, RAMÓN — (1888–1956) Essayist; novelist. *Goya*,

Velázquez, Automoribundia, etc. Invented a new idea of lyric metaphor ("gregueria").

GÓNGORA, LUIS DE — (1561–1627) Baroque poet. *Las soledades, Polifemo.* Also popular poet in short verse forms.

GONZÁLEZ RUANO, CÉSAR — (1903–1965) Journalist, poet. *Baudelaire, Bala de cherche-midi*, etc.

GONZALO DE BERCEO — (1198?–1274?) Perhaps the first known poet in Spanish literature; sang to the Virgin and the saints. "Vida de San Millán," "Vida de Santa Oria," "Vida de Santo Domingo de Silos," "Loores de nuestra Señora, "Milagros de nuestra Señora," etc.

GRACIÁN, BALTASAR ("LORENZO GRACIÁN") — (1601–1658) Jesuit; famous writer; author of *El Criticón.*

IRIARTE, JUAN — (1702–1771) Spanish poet and writer, of the Academia Española.

IRIARTE, TOMÁS DE — (1750–1791) Spanish poet and writer, author of literary fables which gave him tremendous fame.

JARDIEL PONCELA, ENRIQUE — (1901–1952) Humorist, introduced a new style in novels (*Pero, ¿hubo alguna vez once mil vírgenes?*) and plays (*Los ladrones somos gente honrada, Eloisa esta debajo del almendro, Angelina o el honor de un brigadier*, etc.).

JÉRICA, PABLO DE — (1781–1833?) Poet. *Poesías, Ensayos poéticos*, etc.

LAIGLESIA, ALVARO DE — (1922–   ) Humorist; editor of *La Codorniz.* Novelist: *Todos los ombligos son redondos, Qué bien huelen las señoras, Solo se mueren los tontos*, etc.

LARA, ANTONIO DE — See "Tono"

LARRA, MARIANO JOSÉ DE ("FIGARO") — (1809–1837) The first "columnist" in Spanish journalism. With Cadalso and Fernández Flórez, a keen critic of society. *Artículos de costumbres, políticos, sociales*, etc.

LAS CASAS, BARTOLOMÉ DE — (1475–1566) Dominican and bishop. Accused the Spaniards of cruelty to Caribbean Indians in his *Destrucción de las Indias*, and defended the bringing of African Negroes to do the work the indigenous could not perform.

LORCA, FEDERICO GARCIA — (1899–1936) Great poet and playwright. *Romancero gritano, Yerma, Bodas de Sangre, La casa de Bernarda Alba*, etc.

MACHADO, ANTONIO — (1875–1939) Great poet and thinker on the subject of the evils of Spain. *Soledades, Campos de Castilla, Nuevas canciones*, etc.

MACHADO, MANUEL — (1874–1947) Antonio's brother, with a literary grace more Andalusian than Castilian. *Alma, Museo, Los cantares, La guerra literaria*, etc.

MADARIAGA, SALVADOR DE — (1886–   ) Minister, ambassador; lives in England. *Ingleses, franceses y espanoles*, first great comparative study. Historian (*Colón, Bolívar*), novelist.

MARAÑÓN, GREGORIO — (1887–1960) Doctor, historian, professor, essayist; triumphed in every field. *Tres ensayos sobre la vida sexual, Ensayos sobre Don Juan, El Conde Duque de Olivares, Antonio Pérez*, etc.

MESONERO Y ROMANOS, RAMÓN DE — (1803–1882) Writer on Madrid customs. *Panorama matritense, Memorias de un setentón*, etc.

MIHURA, MIGUEL — (1907–   ) Creator of a new kind of humor after the civil war with *La Cordorniz.* Comedy writer: *Ni pobre ni rico sino todo lo contrario* (with Tono), *Sublime decisión, Carlota,* etc.

MINGOTE BARRACHINA, ANGEL ANTONIO — (1919–   ) Most popular cartoonist and humorist. *Historia de la gente, Las palmeras de cartón,* etc.

ORTEGA Y GASSET, JOSÉ — (1883–1955) Great writer, introduced European culture to Spain with the *Revista de Occidente.* Sociologist. *Meditaciones del Quijote, El espectador, La rebelión de las masas,* etc.

ORTEGA Y MUNILLA, JOSÉ — (1856–1922) Novelist and journalist; father of Ortega y Gasset. *La Cigarra,* etc.

PALACIO VALDÉS, ARMANDO — (1853–1938) Very popular novelist among the Spanish middle classes. *Marta y María, José, Riverita, Maximina, La hermana San Sulpicio, La aldea perdida,* etc.

PARDO BAZÁN, EMILIA — (1852–1921) Spanish novelist and critic. Her first work was a critical study of the works of Father Feijóo. *Los pazos de Ulloa, La madre naturaleza, Morriña,* etc.

PASO, ALFONSO — (1926–   ) Very popular and successful comedy writer. *Una bomba llamada Abelardo, Pobres chicas las que tienen que servir,* etc. More than a hundred works performed by the time he was forty.

PEREDA, JOSÉ MARÍA DE — (1833–1906) Novelist of a regionalist and conservative type. *Don Gonzalo González de la Gonzalera, Sotileza, La puchera, Peñas arriba,* etc.

PÉREZ GALDÓS, BENITO — (1843–1920) The greatest Spanish novelist since Cervantes. Had a profound knowledge of Spanish society, especially the bureaucratic society of Madrid. *Tormento; La de Bringas; Miau; Torquemada en la hoguera . . . en el purgaturio . . . y San Pedro . . .* (studies of the avaricious man). Historical novels (*Episodios nacionales,* plays (*Electra*), etc. Praised by the Left; refused by the Right.

QUEVEDO, FRANCISCO GÓMEZ DE — (1580–1645) Satirist and great poet. *Política de Dios, Los sueños, La hora de todos,* and a picaresque novel, *El buscón llamado don Pablos.*

QUINTERO, SERAFÍN ALVAREZ — (1871–1938) Playwright. Comedies of Andalusian customs such as *Malvaloca, Las Flores.*

QUINTERO, JOAQUÍN ALVAREZ — (1873–1944) Playwright; all works written in collaboration with his brother.

RIVAS, DUKE OF — (1791–1865) Diplomat, dramatic poet. *Don Alvaro o la fuerza del sino* (1835) produced the scandal of the new romantic theater. *Lanuza, El moro expósito, Romances históricos,* etc.

ROJAS, FERNANDO DE — (1475?–1541) Converted Jew, probable author of *La Celestina,* which created a new Spanish word.

RUIZ, JOSÉ MARTÍNEZ ("AZORÍN") — (1874–1967) Gave the generation of '98 its name and has been one of its chief exponents in essays, articles and novels. *Alma castellana, Los pueblos, La ruta de Don Quijote, Clásicos y modernos, La voluntad, Doña Inés, Don Juan,* etc. Plays: *Angelita, Old Spain,* etc.

SÁNCHEZ ALBORNOZ Y MENDUIÑA, CLAUDIO — (1893–   ) Politician, historian. *La España musulmana, León en el siglo X,* etc. His controversy with Américao Castro after the latter's *La realidad histórica de España* has been the subject of many comments.

SERNA, VICTOR DE LA — (1896–1953) Journalist. *Viaje por España, Doce viñetas, La poesía trovadoresca y los cantos de payador.*

SOLANA, EZEQUIEL — (1863–   ) Schoolmaster and writer.

TIRSO DE MOLINA — (1571–1648) Pseudonym of Brother Gabriel Téllez. Created the modern type of Don Juan in *El burlador de Sevilla y convidado de piedra.* Other plays: *El vergonzoso en palacio, Don Gil de las calzas verdes.* Theological plays, *El condenado por desconfiado,* etc.

"TONO," ANTONIO DE LARA — (1896–   ) Dramatist and humorist; Mihura's collaborator on *La Codorniz. Rebeco, Crimen pluscuamperfecto* (plays).

UNAMUNO, MIGUEL DE — (1864–1936) The most Spanish of the Spanish intellectuals. University professor, poet, essayist. *Del sentimiento trágico de la vida, Vida de Don Quijote y Sancho Panza, Mi religión y otros ensayos, El Cristo de Velázquez,* etc.

VALERA, JUAN — (1824–1925) Diplomat, essayist, novelist. *Pepita Jiménez, Juanita la larga,* etc.

VALLE INCLÁN, RAMÓN DEL — (1866–1936) Great physical and literary personality. Creator of the Donjuanesque Marquis of Bradomín. *Voces de gesta; Sonata de otoño . . . de estío . . . de invierno . . . de primavera; Tirano banderas;* etc.

VEGA, LOPE DE — (1562–1635) Dramatist and poet. Incredible vitality reflected in his works and love affairs. Founder of the Spanish national drama. *La dama boba, Fuenteove-juna, Las bizarrías de Belisa, El acero de Madrid,* etc.

VILLAESPESA, FRANCISCO — (1877–1936) Poet and playwright. Plays in verse: *El alcazar de las perlas, Aben humeya, La leona de Castilla,* etc.

VILLAMEDIANA, COUNT JUAN DE TASSIS Y PERALTA — (1580–1622) Satirical poet.

ZORRILLA, JOSÉ — (1817–1893) Poet of facile, sonorous verse, very well remembered. His play *Don Juan Tenorio* is still performed successfully every year. His "Oriental" is recited in many Spanish houses.